Clever Folk

Clever Folk
Tales of Wisdom, Wit, and Wonder

Ruthilde M. Kronberg

Illustrated by
Michael Kronberg

1993
LIBRARIES UNLIMITED, INC.
Englewood, Colorado

To my husband, Peter, who has a thousand projects but is always there when I need him, and to Peter, Brenda, Andreas, Michael, Miki, Miriam, Valerie, and Daniel.

LIBRARIES UNLIMITED, INC.
P.O. Box 6633
Englewood, CO 80155-6633

Library of Congress Cataloging-in-Publication Data

Kronberg, Ruthilde, 1930-
    Clever folk : tales of wisdom, wit, and wonder / Ruthilde M. Kronberg ; illustrated by Michael Kronberg.
    x, 151 p. 17x25 cm.
    ISBN 1-56308-139-3
    1. Tales. 2. Tales--Study and teaching. 3. Storytelling.
4. Moral education.   I. Title.
GR76.K76   1993
398.2--dc20   93-4793
                                                  CIP

Contents

Preface ix

Part I: Stories to Tell and Read Aloud

The Stories

The Faithful Wives *(Value: Faithfulness)*
Age 8 and up 5

Mother Holdra's Tonic *(Value: Cooperation)*
Age 6 and up 7

Hideehohee *(Value: Courage)*
Age 8 and up 11

The Giant Who Learned to Love Children
(Values: Responsibility, Cooperation, and Respect)
All ages 17

The Elf's Hat *(Values: Responsibility and Love)*
Age 8 and up 23

The Farmer and the Wolf *(Value: Honesty)*
Age 8 and up 27

The Three Hundred Iron Rods *(Values: Honesty and Respect)*
Older children 30

The King and the Broommaker *(Value: Honesty)*
Older children 32

Hans and Grete, Nineteen Now
(Values: Responsibility and Self-Respect)
Older children 35

Bird Baby Don't Fly *(Values: Respect and Responsibility)*
Older children 41

The Boy Who Called the King a Fool *(Value: Responsibility)*
Older children 47

A Perjurer Is a Liar *(Values: Truthfulness and Responsibility)*
Older children 53

The Bridge Across the Fire *(Value: Compassion)*
Older children 56

Hehheh and the Honey Cakes *(Values: Humanity and Compassion)*
Age 8 and up 57

Hehheh and the Magic Needle *(Value: Self-Esteem)*
Age 8 and up 61

Hehheh and the Fisherman
(Values: Responsibility and Trustworthiness)
Age 8 and up 65

Hehheh and the Hay *(Values: Responsibility and Kindness)*
Age 8 and up 69

Hehheh and the Mayor *(Value: Respect)*
Age 8 and up 72

Part II: Stories to Act Out

The Three Languages *(Values: Courage and Caring)*
Age 8 and up 79

The Elephant and the Monkey *(Values: Cooperation and Respect)*
Younger children 87

The Farmer and the Stork *(Value: Responsibility)*
Older children 93

Kannitverstan *(Value: Humility)*
Age 8 and up 95

A Mother's Advice *(Values: Responsibility and Honesty)*
Age 8 and up 99

The Nobleman and the Carrier *(Values: Respect and Humility)*
Older children 103

The Clever Maid *(Values: Cooperation and Responsibility)*
Age 8 and up 107

The Clever Village Magistrate *(Values: Honesty and Respect)*
Older children 113

The Wicked Judge *(Values: Responsibility and Humanity)*
Older children 119

The Dishonest Innkeeper *(Value: Honesty)*
Older children 122

Part III: Stories That Involve the Audience

Bunny Pink Learns How to Think
(Values: Self-Esteem and Responsibility)
Ages 3-8 131

Old Man Winter and Rabbit Mother
(Values: Responsibility and Perseverance)
Ages 8-10 and a play for ages 6-8 139

Notes on the Stories 147
About the Author and Illustrator 151

Preface

One of the most exciting things that happened at the St. Louis Story-telling Festival 1992 was the inclusion of student storytellers. Here they were, the storytellers of the future, offering a gift to the audience with their beautiful, lovingly prepared tales.

When I was their age, and living in war-torn Germany, a wise teacher, who knew my passionate love for reading, asked me to translate "The Happy Prince" by Oscar Wilde from English into German. She could not have given me a better story. At that time I could easily relate to Wilde's characters, since I too was often sad, hungry, and frightened. As the swallow in the story brought the gifts of the prince to the people, it also brought a gift to me.

Until then studying the English language had been quite a chore for me. But as the story unfolded, and I began to see the beauty of it, I had to know how it ended. I translated the story in record time, and wonder of wonders, I began to like studying the English language. Little did I know that I would end up in America, telling stories in English to thousands of children.

Through the years I have received many story gifts, which helped me to reflect, grow, and mature. One of the joys of my life is to pass them on.

"There is currently a national groundswell crying out for values education," writes Carl Yochum, coordinator of the Personal Responsibility Education Program (PREP) in the Ferguson-Florissant School District of Missouri. "Stories often influence the behavioral patterns of young people and hopefully contribute to many long-range, positive character changes in our children."

When asked to tell stories at the PREP, which teaches honesty, cooperation, courage, kindness, respect, compassion, humanity, and self-esteem, I told many of the stories that are now in this book. Afterward the older students either told or acted out the stories for younger students.

Watching their students teach values through storytelling, and seeing how it increased their self-confidence and polished their public-speaking skills, the teachers became interested in storytelling and asked if they could use my stories. When told that they were my own versions of mostly unknown stories they suggested that I write a book.

There are currently 21 school districts in the greater St. Louis area that use the Personal Responsibility Education Program and, as an important part of it, offer storytelling workshops for teachers. Statistics show that in some schools' referrals to the principal's office have dropped 24 percent and that the number of students who read on or above the national level is rising.

This book is divided into three parts. Part I contains stories that can be read or told to children of various ages. They tell about folks like you and me, and how they solve their problems with wit, intelligence, and courage.

The stories in parts II and III will help children to become storytellers and to pass on what they have learned. Hearing and telling stories from all over the world teaches children that people have similar values, which is particularly important in a country of multiple cultures.

Verna Stassevitch, head mistress of the Wilson School in Clayton, Missouri, says this about the influence of stories on children. "When I am asked by parents, 'What does the school do about moral development in children?' I have an immediate response: We have a storyteller! For more than fifteen years Ruthilde has inspired children, and taught them about the important values of life through her amazing knowledge of myths, tales, legends and stories."

Helping students express their feelings and look for resolution and encouraging them to become storytellers are among the most rewarding things I have done in my life.

Part I
Stories to Tell and Read Aloud

One of the most precious gifts anyone can give to children is to read or tell a well-chosen story. Although my brothers and I were avid readers at an early age, we treasured the times our father read to us. It told us that he enjoyed doing something with us.

Remembering the stories, by Leo Tolstoy, Selma Lagerloef, Werner Bergengruen, Jeremias Gotthelf, and many more, I later realized that all of them taught values. Telling us to be kind and respectful, industrious and helpful was not enough for my father. He chose fascinating stories that made those values desirable to us.

The stories in part I are for a wide variety of ages. They tell of people who are faithful, generous, loving, courageous, smart, honest, and compassionate.

1

Several of the stories in this part feature a recurring character. Long ago when the deities sent messengers to the Earth to give advice to the people and help them grow and mature, a sojourner by the name of Hehheh wandered through the towns and villages of Hessia. Whenever he passed through a community, children and adults would come up to him and ask him to help them solve their problems. No one knew where Hehheh came from or if he had a permanent home somewhere. But everyone trusted him because they knew that he was one of those truly good persons who treated all of God's creatures with respect and love.

Hehheh's wisdom was the commonsense wisdom of the Proverbs, his magic was the magic of dreams, and his humor made people chuckle and talk about him years later. Adults and children alike loved Hehheh because he brought out the good in them and gave them hope and courage to cope with life on this Earth. In order to find the right story for your child or children, read a few stories, or read the "Notes on the Stories," beginning on page 147. It is good to remember that one can adjust a story to different age levels and that children understand by hearing long before they understand by reading.

The Stories

The Faithful Wives

A Story About the Value of Faithfulness

Close to the city of Weinsberg, in Germany, stood long ago the old castle Weibertreu, which means "The Castle of the Faithful Wives." The castle's name was not always Weibertreu. It used to be Castle Weinsberg. But one day a group of faithful women gave the castle its new name.

It happened in the year 1140 when Duke Welf of Bavaria and his men rebelled against King Konrad the Third. The king gathered an army and met the duke's army outside Castle Weinsberg.

Both sides fought fiercely, but the king's men outnumbered the duke's, and he had to retreat to his castle. "We are going to recoup and send Konrad packing," boasted Duke Welf. "We have enough food in this castle, and we can always get more from my villages."

But when food began to get scarce, and his men wanted to use the secret supply road, they found it blocked by the king's soldiers. When there was nothing left but a few sacks of barley, the duke said to his wife, Jutta, "There is no need to let the women and children starve to death. I shall surrender as soon as we have eaten the last bowl of soup."

"What makes you think the king will let us leave the castle?" retorted the duchess. "You and your men will be killed, and we'll be locked up in the dungeon and starve to death."

"Nonsense," replied Duke Welf. "Men do not fight wars against women."

"Men do not fight wars against women, because women would not fight back," cried the duchess furiously. "But while warring, men maim and kill the sons, and the sweethearts, and the husbands of women, and that causes them more pain than a quick death on a battlefield. So do not surrender. If we are all going to die let us die together."

But Jutta's friend Lady Elizabeth did not agree with her. She said, "King Konrad is not a ruthless man. Let me write a petition. If the king grants it, we all will live. If he doesn't, we will pay the cost for our husbands will need to make war."

The following day the king received Lady Elizabeth's petition, which said—

We, the sad and distraught wives of the conquered, humbly beg you to let us and our offspring leave the castle with what we can carry on our backs.

Because King Konrad was indeed a just man he granted the petition, but the proud husbands balked when they found out what the women wanted to carry on their backs. Tears, screaming, begging, wailing, hugs, kisses—the wives tried everything to make them agree, and finally won.

The following morning a long row of wives climbed awkwardly down the steep mountain path, each carrying her husband on her back. The red-faced, feisty duke was clinging with all his might to the back of his tiny duchess. Tall and slender Lady Elizabeth clutched her toddler's hand, while carrying her embarrassed-looking husband, Lord Rudolph, on her shoulders. Delicate Lady Ursula was almost buried under the weight of her husky spouse, while the broad-hipped, broad-shouldered Lady Theresa had no problem carrying her twin babies and her robust husband down the path.

When King Konrad saw his insolent, arrogant, haughty opponents clinging desperately to their wives' backs, their faces red with embarrassment, he began to laugh like he had never laughed before.

"By Jove," said he, "I thought the women meant to carry their treasures on their backs."

"To a loving woman her husband is her treasure," said his queen, who had come to visit him after the battle was over.

"You are not going to grant them their lives!?" shouted his brother, the sour-faced Duke Friedrick von Hohenstaufen, angrily. "Remember, they rebelled against you and might rebel again."

"I have granted their petition and I will not go back on my word," replied the king. "But from now on this castle shall be called Castle Weibertreu. The Castle of the Faithful Wives."

History tells us that the king's decision was a wise one. The duke of Bavaria recognized his greatness, and he and his men became the king's loyal friends.

The End

Mother Holdra's Tonic

A Story About the Value of Cooperation

In the olden times, when things were not at all that good for many, there lived a poor widow who had seven children. Even though the widow worked day and night, there was never enough to chew and swallow for all of them. One day she sent her oldest daughter, Katrinele, to gather mushrooms in the forest.

When the girl came home, her basket was only half filled, and she said, "Mammele, do not get upset. I didn't spend all my time in the forest. I went to the village to look for a job, and I found one at old Hendrick's farm."

"Good heavens," cried the poor widow. "How could you do a thing like that? He is the worst miser who ever walked on God's earth."

"Mammele," replied Katrinele, "no one else would hire me. Old Hendrick was the only one who promised me three gulden at the end of the year, provided I did my work to his satisfaction."

"Ha!" cried the distraught mother. "There you have it. Mark my words. All year long he'll make you labor like a slave, and the day before he pays you he will find fault with your work and cheat you out of your wages. Oh Katrinele, oh Katrinele, why did you not ask me before you went to him?"

"Mammele, I knew you would never have given me permission to go. Listen to me, this way I no longer have to take away bread from the mouths of the little ones. Even if he cheats me, he cannot deny me food while I work for him."

"That is true," replied the poor widow. "But the little food I give you, I give you with love. The food you will eat at his house will be seasoned with your tears."

"Food is food," replied Katrinele, and the next day she started to work for Hendrick.

Oh, what a horrible job it was! Not a moment's peace. Screaming and fussing all day long and never a word of praise. And the food—it was terrible. Watery onion soup with not a speck of meat in it, three times a day.

Hunger would again have been Katrinele's daily companion but for Grumble, the best milk-cow on the farm. Grumble had as mean a temper as Hendrick. It took two people to milk her: one to hold her tail and one to do the milking. It was usually Katrinele's job to hold the tail, and many a kick she got when she held it.

But there was a reward for the nasty job. Liese the milkmaid was so skilled at milking that twice a day she squirted milk into her own and Katrinele's mouth. That kept the girls' strength up, but of course it had to

7

be done behind Hendrick's back. Had he found out that they were drinking a few cups of his precious milk, he would have accused them of stealing, and sent them away.

Oh yes, times were hard for the poor, but sometimes a bit of luck comes even to them. One day Katrinele was out in the forest gathering kindling wood when suddenly she heard a strange sound. "Meow, meow." She looked around, and what did she see? A tiny white cat.

Eya yey, what was Katrinele to do? Surely she could not pick the little cat up and bring her to old Hendrick's house, but neither could she leave her in the forest. A fox would come and eat her. I'll take her with me and hide her, and find a place for her as soon as I can, thought Katrinele, and she put the little creature into her pocket.

That evening she hid the little cat in the attic room that she shared with Liese, but finding a place was easier said than done. Most of the village people had more than enough cats. How Katrinele managed to save bits and pieces of food for the little cat I do not know, but one day Liese left the attic door open and the little cat came downstairs. Just as Katrinele ran to catch her old Hendrick entered the house.

"Oh, you wicked girl," cried he. "How dare you keep a cat in my house. I hate cats. You are fired and your wages will pay for the food you have stolen for her."

"But old Hendrick, the little cat ate only scraps, and they didn't cost a penny," cried Katrinele. "I'll make it up to you."

"You heard what I said," replied the cruel man. "Take that cat and go."

Katrinele cried all the way home. My mother was right all along, she thought. Oh, what will she say when I come home without my wages and with a stray cat to feed? Did Katrinele receive a word of reproach from her Mammele? Not one. Only hugs and kisses, and her brothers and sisters shouted with joy when they saw the little cat. They named her Runaway and loved her dearly.

But Runaway stayed only three days with the family. On the evening of the fourth day she walked up to the door and began to meow in the most pitiful way. "Something is bothering Runaway," said the children, and they tried to pick her up and cuddle her. But the little cat strained away from them and began to meow again. Suddenly there was a knock on the door.

When Katrinele opened the door she found a tiny woman on the doorstep. No bigger than a two-year-old, dressed in a brown cloak, she said with a silvery voice, "I am looking for a tiny white cat. Have you by any chance seen her?"

"Oh, yes," replied Katrinele happily. "Come on in, she is right here." The minute the tiny woman stepped into the house the little cat rushed toward her and jumped into her arms.

"Oh you dear little Runaway," cried the tiny woman. "Must you always run away? I searched and searched, and if I had not heard your little voice tonight I would have thought you dead. How did you end up here?"

"Please sit down, and I will tell you what happened," said Katrinele kindly, and she ran and fetched a little footstool. Mammele insisted on bringing her a tiny cup of tea, and when everyone was comfortable Katrinele told the tiny woman what had happened.

"You lost your job because of my runaway kitten," said the tiny woman after Katrinele had finished her tale.

"She is better off without it," said the widow.

"I know," replied Katrinele wistfully, "but I would have liked to help Mammele put food on the table instead of eating it."

"There must be a better way to get food on your table," muttered the tiny woman, and she got up from her footstool and started to walk around the house. Suddenly her eyes fell upon a bowl filled with elderberries, which the children had picked to make juice.

A smile crinkled up her tiny face and she said, "As soon as the sun rises look at your windowsill and you will find a recipe to make a good livelihood. Now be so kind and open the door for me. They call me Mother Holdra. I belong to the Elf family, and Runaway and I usually don't visit with humans."

Katrinele ran to open the door for Mother Holdra, and she and her little cat walked off into the nearby forest. The following morning the whole family looked at their windowsill and found a piece of birch bark. On it, written in the tiniest spidery script, was a recipe for a tonic to be made from elderberries, honey, and other healing herbs.

Because all the ingredients grew in the nearby forest, Mammele was soon concocting the tonic from all the herbs and berries the children had gathered. The following day she filled several of her crocks and took them to the market. That day only a few people bought her tonic, but a week later a lot of people were waiting for her.

"We heard about your wonderful tonic," they said. "Where in the world did you get the recipe?" The widow told them where it came from, and that day she sold all of her crocks within an hour. By the end of the year people were coming from near and far to buy the tonic, and the widow grew so busy she hired all of the poor folks in the village, including Liese, to work for her.

The birch bark recipe stayed in the family for hundreds of years until one day it crumbled from old age. But to this day people in Germany love to drink Mother Holdra's tonic, and should you ever go there you may want to try it, too.

The End

❖

Hideehohee

A Story About the Value of Courage

In a little tree house in a forest lived a Father and a Mother Elf who had fourteen children. It was a perfect place to raise a family, and they thought they would always live there. But one day a couple of trolls moved into their neighborhood, and soon after the elf parents realized they had to leave.

Elf father and Elf mother would not have minded having trolls for neighbors. They firmly believed that the world was big enough for all kinds of creatures, but these trolls had an unusual habit. Instead of eating berries and nuts like other trolls, they loved to eat bug sausage.

Every day Troll-man roamed through the forest, gathering worms and caterpillars, lizards, and whatever else he could find, and when his sack was full he took it home to Troll-hag. Without a twinge of pity Troll-hag would sprinkle salt and pepper all over the ill-fated, little creatures and stuff them into a big, leathery sausage skin. Then she and Troll-man would boil the sausage and eat it.

Since trolls are known to be very nearsighted the Elf parents became worried that one day one of their precious little ones might be mistaken for a bug and end up in a troll sausage. In order to forestall such a tragedy, Elf father went out and hired twenty Jack Rabbits to take his family and his household goods to an elf colony, where they would be much safer.

Since it was unwise to let all of the rabbits go at once, Elf father told each how to find his way to the elf colony. Unfortunately, the rabbit who was carrying his second oldest son, Hideehohee, was a rather giddy creature. He ran in the wrong direction, and when he found that he had lost his way, he was so embarrassed he tossed Hideehohee off his back and ran off into the forest.

When the rabbit didn't come back Hideehohee decided to find his own way to the elf colony. He got up and began to walk. But as soon as he came to a clearing, a huge bird swooped out of the sky and grabbed him with his talons. Just as they were about to disappear in the clouds, Milia, an old woman who was picking berries that day, looked up and saw what was happening. She picked up an earth clod and threw it at the bird.

Part of the earth clod hit the bird's talons, and he let go of Hideehohee, but now Hideehohee was falling. Old Milia tried to catch him, but she was too slow, and poor little Hideehohee landed right in the middle of a huge thornbush. It is true that the thornbush kept him from breaking his neck, but there were so many sharp thorns in his backside that he looked like a porcupine.

It took old Milia almost an hour before she had removed them all, and when she was done Hideehohee was in no shape to travel. All he could do was lie on his tummy and suffer. Fortunately old Milia had a kind heart. She took him home and cared for him, promising all the while that she would take him back to the forest as soon as he was well.

But when her husband, Grauslick, found out what she was about to do he said, "Don't be a silly goose, Milia. You spent all your time caring for the little imp, the least he can do is help us to make some extra money. I have always wanted to have my own chickens. I'll go and buy a carton of baby chicks, and he can raise them."

Hideehohee would not have minded raising baby chicks, but those baby chicks had very small brains. They were supposed to stay in the carton next to the warm stove, but they loved to jump over the carton top and dirty up the kitchen floor.

Since Grauslick hated a dirty kitchen floor, Hideehohee had to move in with the chicks and hang onto their legs whenever they wanted to jump out. It was a terrible job, and Hideehohee couldn't wait until they were big enough to go out into the yard. At least then he wouldn't have to stay in the carton all day.

How glad he was when they were finally able to go outside, but instead of staying in the yard those little chicks began to dart out into the street. Nothing could make them realize that streets were made for wagons, and not for baby chicks. All day long Hideehohee had to rush after them and bring them back to safety.

It really was a dangerous job. Hideehohee himself was so small that most of the drivers of the wagons could not see him. Quite often he came so close to being run over that he began to wonder if he was ever going to see his parents again. But he kept on hoping that sooner or later he would have a chance to leave, and one day that chance came.

On a fine afternoon, after he had chased the chicks for hours, Hideehohee found a ten-dollar bill right in the middle of the street. When he came inside he gave it to old Milia and said, "Buy yourself something nice, Aunty. You deserve it." But that evening Grauslick was in one of his table-banging moods. Anxious to please him, Milia showed him the ten-dollar bill and said, "Little Hideehohee found it and gave it to me."

That was the last time she saw the ten-dollar bill. Grauslick snatched it from her hand and roared, "Ha, why didn't I think of that. The little imp is closer to the ground than we. He should not waste his time on those dumb chicks. I'll take care of the little critters, and make him look for dollar bills."

Looking for dollar bills seemed easier than watching baby chicks. During the first three days Hideehohee found one five-dollar bill and three one-dollar bills. But people don't go around dropping dollar bills. When they lose one they try extra hard not to lose another one. Soon Hideehohee was finding only quarters and dimes, and one evening he came home empty-handed.

This made Grauslick so mad he spanked Hideehohee with a Popsicle stick and locked him in the storage room. No one had ever spanked Hideehohee. Too sad to cry he made up a song.

I'm Hideehohee, I'm Hideehohee.
I must go and find my family.
I always will be sad, I never will be glad
Until I find my Mom and Dad.

Poor Hideehohee, would he ever find his family? Not by sitting in a storage room and singing sad songs. He had to help himself, and the first thing to do was to escape from Grauslick. Hideehohee looked around and saw that the window was open. That was good news. The bad news was that the window was six feet above the ground, and he would break his neck if he tried to jump.

If he wanted to escape he would need a rope, and Grauslick didn't keep his ropes in the storage room. He kept his ropes in the barn. But it didn't take the smart little fellow a lot of time to find a rope. He waited till the house was quiet, and then he took all of the shoelaces out of Grauslick's old shoes. After he had knotted them into a long rope, he fastened it to the window latch and slid down into the garden.

Luck was with him that night. As he stumbled through the darkness he met a friendly raccoon, who took him to the forest. It felt wonderful to be back, but being in the forest had its own dangers. There were all those wild creatures, and Hideehohee was so small and could be so easily swallowed.

Hideehohee tried to be careful. He found himself a hidey-hole, and went out only when he needed food and water. But even that was not safe. One day a ruthless pole cat sneaked up on him and was just about to jump on him when a bird warned him, yelling "Popp, popp, popp, popp, popp, popp, popp-popp, a pole cat, a pole cat, a pole cat."

A pole cat! Hideehohee didn't turn to look, he just ran like he never ran before. By the time he reached his hidey-hole he was so frightened that he thought he would never go out and search for food again. But hunger hurts, and as he sat there thinking of all the good things he used to eat at his parents' house, he wondered if there was anyone more miserable than he.

It didn't take long before he found out that there were lots of creatures more miserable than he. Only a few hours later he heard someone whimper. It sounded so sad that Hideehohee ignored his own fears and crept out of his hole to find out who was in trouble.

He didn't have to look far. About ten feet from his place he found a half-starved bat who could not fly because she had a big tear in her wing. Now quite a lot of folks won't touch bats because they think they are ugly.

But Hideehohee had been taught to respect all creatures. He examined the wing, and as he wondered how he could fix it Grauslick's shoelaces came to his mind.

Grinning from ear to ear, Hideehohee found himself a long, strong thorn and used it to poke tiny holes along each side of the tear on the bat's wing. Then he took a few strands of his own hair and laced the torn sides together, just as one laces a shoe. By the time he was done the wing was as good as new, and no one was happier than the bat. She couldn't find enough words to thank Hideehohee, and in order to show the world how glad she was, she flew over the forest and screeched,

> Whee, hee, whee, you all listen to me,
> If you're in pain, go to Hideehohee.
> He made me well, he fixed my wing.
> I'm sure he can mend most anything.

Soon injured animals came from near and far. Hideehohee fixed broken bird wings and pulled thorns out of bear paws. He put lost moles back into their holes and pulled rotten teeth out of wolves' jaws. He glued broken turtle shells with pitch and fixed the torn webs between hundreds of duck feet.

Helping others made him so happy he forgot his own sorrow, and one day, much to his own surprise, he found himself singing.

> I'm Hideehohee, I'm Hideehohee.
> One day I might find my family.
> I am no longer sad.
> Helping others makes me glad.
> My life is not at all that bad.

Indeed he was leading a happy life. In return for his care the animals looked out for him. He could walk anywhere in the forest without fear, and one day when he was least expecting it, a raven, whose broken wing he had set, alighted next to him and cawed, "Caw, caw, caw, Hideehohee, jump on my back. I think I found your elf colony."

Hideehohee could not believe his ears. He jumped on the raven's back and sure enough, as they flew over the forest he began to recognize his old neighborhood. Eager to see things better, Hideehohee tried to stand up and peek over the raven's head. By the time the raven realized what Hideehohee was doing it was too late. Hideehohee had lost his balance and was once again tumbling through the air.

This time he didn't fall into a thornbush, but instead fell into a deep ditch, and that could have been the end of his life. But the wind had blown thousands of autumn leaves into the ditch, and Hideehohee fell on a soft cushion. Not one limb was broken, but the fall had knocked the breath out of him. He never heard the caws of the faithful raven who searched for him for hours and finally flew home, telling all the animals that Hideehohee had disappeared.

While the animals were mourning his disappearance, Hideehohee slept like a baby, and when the sun rose he started to climb out of the ditch. But just as he reached the top, Troll-man came around and swooped him into his huge bug sack. There he was among a lot of crying little creatures, unable to do a thing.

As soon as Troll-man got home he emptied the sack into a vat and yelled, "Troll-hag, get the sausage meat ready while I'll get the water to boil." Smacking her lips Troll-hag put the usual amount of salt and pepper all over the bugs and Hideehohee, and stuffed them into a big, leathery sausage skin.

In the meantime Troll-man tried to get the kettle of water to boil, but a strong wind was blowing, and it took him longer than usual. When Troll-hag saw that it would take awhile until breakfast was ready she sat down in her rocking chair and fell sound asleep.

Soon she was snoring so loudly that Hideehohee could hear her from inside the sausage skin, and he thought, Since I am still alive and kicking I better find a way to get out before she wakes up again. He began to grope around, and before long he found a short stick. Since trolls have iron teeth Troll-hag never bothered to remove the sticks that her husband had picked up along with the bugs, and now the stick came in handy. Hideehohee took it and rammed it with all his might against the tough sausage skin. Soon there was a hole big enough for him and the bugs to climb out.

As they were scurrying around trying to find a way out of the trolls' cave, a mouse popped out of her hole and showed them a mole tunnel, which led all the way to the river. It was wonderful to jump into the cool water and wash off the salt and pepper. While they were splashing happily about Troll-man came into the cave to get the sausage. When he saw nothing but an empty skin he shook Troll-hag until her teeth rattled and shouted, "Did you eat the sausage meat, you greedy old toad?"

"I didn't," yelled Troll-hag, and she kicked his shins so hard he jumped three feet high.

"Stop kicking me," yelled Troll-man.

"Stop shaking me," yelled Troll-hag, but neither of them stopped, and they shook and kicked each other for the rest of the day. What a way to live.

In the meantime Hideehohee came out of the river and sat in the sun to dry his clothes. Suddenly a rabbit came hopping along. He took one look at Hideehohee and cried, "Is that you Hideehohee, or am I seeing a ghost?"

"I'm Hideehohee," replied Hideehohee. "Who are you?"

"I am the rabbit who deserted you," replied the rabbit. "I have searched for you ever since. I can't tell you how happy I am to see you. There were times I was sure you had died because I could not find you anywhere.

Please jump on my back. By now I know the way to the elf colony and I'll take you there."

Hideehohee stared at the rabbit. Could what he said be true? It was so wonderful, it simply had to be true. No one could make up a story like that. Without further questioning he jumped on the rabbit's back, and sure enough, the rabbit took him straight to the elf colony.

Twelve long months had passed, and Hideehohee had changed so much that his own father didn't recognize him when he opened the door in response to his knock. Too moved to say anything, Hideehohee began to sing.

> I'm Hideehohee, I'm Hideehohee.
> I finally found my family.
> Now I always will be glad,
> I never will be sad,
> Because I found my Mom and Dad.

Ah, I wish I could have been there. What a reunion, what a day. Happiness like that takes my breath away. They talked and hugged and hugged and talked, and after Hideehohee had told his story he said to his parents, "Mama and Dad, if you hadn't taught me to reach out to others, I might never have seen you again."

The End

The Giant Who Learned to Love Children

A Story About the Values of Responsibility, Cooperation, and Respect

As recently as eight hundred years ago there still lived somewhere in Schwabia a giant named Helming. Helming was a very lonesome giant. He had no other giants to keep him company, and although the cave he lived in was lined with precious stones, it was damp and dark.

To break the monotony of his days, Helming spent many hours in front of his cave watching the people in the valley. He saw them living in warm, comfortable houses and sturdy castles, and one day he said to himself, "This cave is not fit to live in. Why don't I build myself a castle and be comfortable?"

The next day he began to break stones off the mountain and started to build a wall. But, being a giant, he did not know the art of cutting stones and fitting them together. Toward evening his wall collapsed, and one of its huge rocks crushed Helming's big toe.

It took the poor giant quite a while before he was able to hobble back to his cave, and while he was bandaging his toe he decided to hire the people in the valley to build him a castle. The following day he limped to the mountain opposite his cave and yelled at the top of his voice,

> Holdrihohou I have a message for you.
> If you build me a castle fit for my size,
> Double wages will be your prize.

The next day was a busy day for the giant Helming. Stonemasons, carpenters, locksmiths, roofers, and turners came from near and far to offer their services.

When all of them were assembled Helming greeted them and said, "I want my castle to be the finest in the land. If I find everything to my liking when the castle is finished, each of you—master, journeyman, and apprentice—will get an additional bonus of one hundred gold pieces."

The craftsmen were speechless. None of them ever had an offer like that. They chose the best among themselves to be in charge, and soon the building site was as busy as a beehive. Men and beasts worked tirelessly, while the giant sat in front of his cave and watched and shouted directions.

After seven long years the workmen were able to dismantle the scaffolding, and three years later the inside of the castle was done.

It was a wonderful castle. The craftsmen felt proud as they walked with Helming through the tall and spacious rooms. From the coal bin in the cellar to the big, hand-hewn beams in the attic, everything spoke of their careful work. They were already thinking of what to do with the extra hundred gold pieces when Helming looked out of the dormer window and discovered that there was no flagpole.

Now Helming was a good-natured giant, but like all giants he had a quick temper. He pointed to the bare eaves and shouted, "Where is the flagpole? I gave instructions to have a flagpole. Where is it? I won't pay an extra penny until I get my flagpole."

The craftsmen looked at each other, they looked out of the dormer window, they looked at each other again. The giant was right, there was no flagpole. What were they to do? They began to argue among themselves, each blaming the other for the missing flagpole.

Finally the master blacksmith spoke up and said, "All our silly blaming and arguing won't put a flagpole on the eaves. I suggest that the master turner make one, and we find a way to get it up there." The master turner ran to his shed in the courtyard, found himself a fine piece of wood, and turn-lathed a smooth, shiny flagpole.

All that needed to be done was to put the flagpole in place, but alas, the scaffolding had been taken down three years ago. The only way to put up the flagpole was to climb up the shutters of the dormer window and nail it from there to the eaves. But who in the world would dare to do such a death-defying job? One wrong move, one strong gust of wind could mean death.

Once again the arguments started, and once again the master blacksmith came up with an idea. "Let's reach into our pockets and fill up a sack with ducats for the one who will be willing to risk his life," said he, and everyone followed his advice. But the fish weren't biting that day. No one wanted to die rich.

In the meantime Helming began to grumble again. "I want my flagpole. Isn't there anyone among you who has the courage to put up my flagpole?"

"I do," said a young journeyman by the name of Pieter. "But only if the master blacksmith will give me permission to marry his daughter Celia." The master blacksmith was not too happy about Pieter's request. Pieter had nothing to offer but his craft and his willingness to work. However, the giant's threats were looming overhead so he said, "If you manage to get the flagpole up on those eaves and stay unharmed you may marry my daughter." Everybody cheered, and Pieter took the flagpole and walked up the castle steps.

When Helming saw him coming he asked, "Aren't you afraid that you might fall?"

"I am afraid," replied Pieter. "But if I survive I will be able to marry the girl I love, and if I die I will be in God's hands."

"You are braver than all the riffraff out there," laughed the giant. "I'll come along and see what you can do."

When they came to the attic the young craftsman leaned the long flagpole against the window frame. Then he put four strong nails into his work apron and began to climb onto the windowsill.

While holding onto the window frame, he leaned as far out as he could and loosened one of the shutter clasps. After pulling the heavy shutter toward the window, he put his feet into the giant-sized louvers and began to climb to the top. Suddenly a gust of wind swept across the mountain range, and the heavy shutter began to swing back and forth.

Hoping that the wind would soon die down Pieter held on for dear life, but the wind increased, and soon he was being tossed back and forth like a ship in an ocean storm.

Just as his strength was beginning to ebb, the giant appeared at the dormer window. He pulled in the shutter, grabbed Pieter by his waist, and lifted him way up to the eaves. Without glancing into the depth below Pieter reached for the flagpole and nailed it in its place.

When the last nail was in the wall, the craftsmen cheered so loudly that folks in the valley heard it and came running. When all the cheering was over, the giant got his money sack and everyone got their promised bonus.

Only Pieter received nothing. When it was his turn to be paid the giant said, "Go and marry Celia, and then return and live with me in this castle. I don't have a son of my own, and I would like you and your wife to take care of me when I get old."

Pieter and Celia were glad to live with the giant, but the first months were not easy. When Helming sneezed all the dishes blew off the table. When he stomped through the kitchen the pots and pans fell off the shelves.

That gnawed-off bones didn't belong underneath the table and that one didn't spit on the floor was news to him. Helming could also be very stubborn when he wanted something his way and Pieter wanted it different. Sometimes he and Pieter had shouting matches, which had Celia and the people in the valley worried.

All that changed when Celia had her first little son. No one in the whole wide world could have ever foreseen that the big rough and tough giant Helming could be so gentle. At first he didn't dare to touch little Niels for fear he would break his bones. "He's just like a little bird," Helming would whisper. "I'm afraid I'll crush him with my big, old, clumsy fingers."

In time he got more confidence, and by the time Niels's sister Eril came along, the giant Helming was the best grandfather Celia and Pieter could have wished for their children. When the children were tiny and screamed, he rocked them and sang to them. When they were sick, he, who used to stomp around like an elephant, walked as silently as a kitten.

As Niels and Eril grew bigger Helming played with them all day long. He lifted them up so they could look into bird nests and see the little fledglings. He bent fruit trees down so they could eat the juiciest cherries. In winter he carried them to the top of the mountain so they could ride their sleds down into the valley.

He taught them not to fear anything, but to still be cautious, and when they were old enough to go to school, he took them there. Soon all their friends begged to play with the old giant, and he became a familiar sight, walking across the mountains with a bunch of children sitting on his head and shoulders, and peeking out of his pockets.

In return for all the fun, he liked to have the children comb his unruly hair and recite their lessons to him. Hearing what they had learned in school gave Helming so much pleasure that the children vied with each other to share their knowledge with him.

It was a life filled with love, joy, and learning, and Helming grew very old among his friends. He lived to see Niels and Eril's children, and when his time to die arrived, he said, "The happiest day in my life was when I learned to love children."

The End

The Elf's Hat

A Story About the Values of Responsibility and Love

Long ago there lived a man who had two sons and one daughter. No one knows why he only loved the daughter and not the sons, but the poor boys had a hard time in their father's house. All day long the old man scolded, "You good-for-nothing rascals, you do not deserve the food you eat. Why am I burdened with such aimless dimwits?"

When the daughter tried to speak well on her brothers' behalf she too got a scolding, "You silly goose, you look at those unruly louts with rose-colored glasses. Mind my words, they'll never amount to anything."

One evening, after a particularly nasty day, the older brother sighed, "I think I have to go and get an elf's hat."

"Why would you want an elf's hat?" asked the younger brother.

"Anet the Goosegirl told me about some elves who live inside the Hirtzig Mountain," replied the older brother. "Their magic hats make them invisible to men. But should a man get hold of an elf's hat, all elves become visible to him, and they will grant him anything he asks for in order to get the hat back."

"If the elves are invisible to men how do you expect to get hold of a hat?" asked the youngest brother.

"Anet says that during the day the elves mine silver and gold inside the mountain, but in the evening they come out and play on the mountain top. One of their favorite games is to hurl their hats high up into the sky and count how many times they can spin around before the hat falls back into their hands. If I could get an elf hat while it's out of an elf's hands, I would ask him to make a potion that would make father love us."

"Could a woman try to get a hat?" asked the sister.

"I suppose she could," replied the brother. "But I wouldn't advise it. If I tried to snatch a hat and failed, the elves would swarm all over me and drag me to their gold mines, and I wouldn't want that to happen to a woman."

"I wouldn't want that to happen to anyone," cried the sister. "Please don't go. I couldn't stand it if you ended up in their mines."

"Working in the gold mines cannot be worse than living with father," replied the older brother. "The more I think about it the more I want to go and get a hat. Please don't try to stop me."

He left the following morning and arrived on the mountain just as the moon was rising in the sky. After eating a piece of bread he brought along he lay down and pretended to be sound asleep. Soon he heard some singing. He blinked his right eye and saw a group of hatless little elves, throwing their hats high up into the air, singing,

> When we take off our hats, we can be seen,
> When we put them back on, we disappear from the scene.
> Dudle-lum-dum-dum, let's watch out for bats,
> And take good care of our magic hats.

Suddenly, one of the hats fell on the older brother's knee. He sat up quickly and tried to grab it. But it's owner was faster than he. He jumped on the older brother's knee, snatched the hat, and yelled, "Ho! Ho! There is a thief in our midst."

"Let's put the rogue into our gold mines," shrieked hundreds of little voices, and hundreds of invisible elves swarmed all over the older brother, and bound him, and tied him, and led him to their gold mines.

At home the younger brother and the sister waited in agony for his return. When they finally had to tell their father that their brother might never come home again, they expected him to be very angry. But the father just laughed and scoffed, "I knew it, I knew it. As soon as the scoundrel is old enough to be of help he runs away. Mark my words, it won't take long before he will find out what the world is like, and when he comes back begging for food, I'll tell him where the carpenter left a hole in the house and what it is for."

"He doesn't care if we live or die," sighed the younger brother, and he left the following day to look for his brother. He too arrived at the mountain just as the moon rose, and lay down in the grass. Soon after, the elves arrived, and, as before, some of them began to throw their hats up into the air, singing,

> When we take off our hats, we can be seen,
> When we put them back on, we disappear from the scene.
> Dudle-lum-dum-dum, let's watch out for bats,
> And take good care of our magic hats.

The younger brother waited until a hat fell right on his chest. But when he tried to reach for the hat the same thing happened, and he too ended up in the gold mines.

When the younger brother didn't return, the sister was inconsolable. She could not eat, she could not sleep, all she could do was sit by the window and weep. One day the father got terribly mad and yelled, "Why are you crying like a condemned soul? You are lucky your brothers ran away. When I die you will inherit all I own, and those hoodlums won't have a chance to squander and waste everything I've worked for."

"My brothers would not have squandered everything you worked for, and they didn't run away either," cried the sister angrily. "They went to the elves who live in the Hirtzig Mountain, hoping to find a potion that would make you love them."

"They went to find a potion that would make me love them?" stammered the father.

"They did," replied the sister. "And now I am leaving too. I'm afraid they ended up in the elves' gold mines, and I'm going to try to get them out."

"I forbid you to go," thundered the father.

"I care for my brothers more than I care for anyone else in the world," said the sister, and before her father could stop her, she ran out of the house, all the way to the mountain.

When she arrived, she lay down on the grass and waited. Everything happened as before. Little hats began to fly, and squeaky little voices began to sing,

> When we take off our hats we can be seen,
> When we put them back on, we disappear from the scene.
> Dudle-lum-dum-dum, let's watch out for bats,
> And take good care of our magic hats.

Very soon a hat fell on the sister's knee, but she didn't touch it. The next hat fell on her arm. Again she didn't touch it. More hats fell on her head and shoulders, but she waited until a hat fell right into her hand.

"Hurrah, I got myself an elf hat," shouted the sister, and she jumped to her feet and held the hat way above the heads of the now visible little elves.

"Give it back to me," begged its little owner.

"Give it back to him," pleaded the rest of the elves. "If you give it back to him we'll grant you anything you ask for."

"First you must bring my brothers to me," said the sister sternly.

When the brothers came out of the mountain and saw their sister they began to weep and they cried, "Oh sister dear, you should have stayed at home. Now you too will have to work for the elves."

"Oh no I won't," laughed the sister, and she began to sing,

> When I take off my hat, I will be seen,
> When I put it back on I disappear from the scene.
> Dudle-dum, dudle-dum, watch out for bats.
> I will take good care of my magic hat.

"You have an elf's hat?" cried the brothers.

"Yes I do," cried the sister, "and now I shall ask my little, hatless elf to make a potion so our father will love you."

"Oiweih, oiweih," cried the elf whose hat she had taken. "We can heal a man's illness with our potions, but we have no potions to make a man love his children. Love for others must come from the heart."

"Then we will stay here," said the sister. "Our father hates my brothers so much they can't possibly return to him."

"You need to be with your own kind," said the elf, "What if we give your brothers the gold they mined. Then they can live on their own and won't have to endure their father's wrath any longer."

"That is an excellent idea," replied the sister.

"I'm glad you think so," chuckled the elf, and he ran and fetched two good sized bags of pure mountain gold and handed them to the brothers. Happy that her brothers could now live on their own the sister gave the elf his hat, but before he popped it on his head and became invisible again, he put a diamond as big as her fist into her hand and said, "If all people were as loving as you we wouldn't have to wear our hats."

While all these wonderful things were happening to his children the father sat in his silent home. Suddenly it hit him like lightning that he was all alone, and would be alone for the rest of his life. He began to pace the floor, moaning and groaning, "My children, my children, what am I going to do without my children?"

When he realized that the moaning and groaning wouldn't bring them back, he said to himself, "I have acted like a fool, and hopefully it is not too late to change." He grabbed his walking stick and hurried toward the Hirtzig Mountain. It was a long journey for an old man, and by the time he reached the first slope he had to sit down from sheer exhaustion.

Suddenly, he saw some people coming down the mountain. As they drew nearer he realized they were his children. He got up and hobbled toward them.

"Father, father," cried the sister. "What are you doing here?"

"I came to ask my sons' forgiveness, and I hope it is not too late," stammered the old man.

"It is not too late," cried the brothers, and they ran and embraced their father. Tears flowed freely, but they were not tears of pain and frustration, they were tears of joy and gratitude.

Afterward, the father and his children went home and started a new life, and let's hope that they did just fine.

The End

The Farmer and the Wolf

A Story About the Value of Honesty

A farmer and his wife decided to slaughter their pig for New Year's Day, but the trough in which the pig needed to be scraped was old and leaky. "I must make a new trough," said the farmer, and he took his saw and his ax and went into the forest.

There he felled a tree, cut it to size, and began to whittle a trough. When the trough was almost finished the farmer saw a wolf coming his way. He quickly overturned the trough and hid underneath it. Thinking that the trough was the trunk of a fallen tree, the wolf sat down on it. Soon a fox joined him, and a moment later a bear and a rabbit arrived.

"Greetings to you, my friends," said the wolf. "What do you plan to eat on New Year's Day? Maybe we all can feast together."

"I shall steal some of the teacher's honey," announced the bear. "I found a way to get into his storeroom."

"The mayor still has some very fine cabbage heads in his garden," chuckled the rabbit. "I already scratched a hole underneath his fence, so it will be easy for me to get them."

"Six fine geese are waiting for me," laughed the fox. "The miser who lives at the end of the village road was too stingy to fix the door of his henhouse. One good push will get me inside, and the geese will be mine."

"Nothing less than one fine pig shall be my repast," bragged the wolf. "I know of a farmer who is going to kill one soon, and I am going to beat him to it."

"Hmm," mumbled the farmer, underneath the trough. "Maybe I can beat you to it, Master Grayskin."

As soon as the animals were gone the farmer ran home and said to his wife, "Quick, put a kettle full of boiling water on the windowsill above the pigsty, and kick it with all your might when I yell 'Kick the bucket.' " Then he went to the pigsty and opened the door slightly.

As soon as it grew dark the wolf came running and pushed his way into the pigsty. But just as he was about to jump on the pig, the door closed with a bang. "Oh no," groaned the wolf, and he began to search for another way out. Suddenly the door opened again.

I better get out of here before the door closes again, thought the wolf, and he ran out. But before he could get away he heard a voice yell, "Kick the bucket," and a stream of hot water hit his pelt.

Oh, how it hurt. While the wolf limped back into the forest the farmer rushed ahead of him and hid once again under his trough. Soon the bear

and the rabbit and the fox appeared. They greeted each other and sat on the trough and waited.

After a while the wolf came limping along. Moaning pitifully he sat next to the bear, but because it was dark none of the other animals could see what was bothering him.

"Before we start our feast let us relate what happened to each of us," said the bear. "I had no trouble getting my pot of honey, and you can all have a mouthful."

"It was easy to get the cabbage," laughed the rabbit. "You are welcome to eat as much as you want."

"My six geese are laying behind a bush, waiting to be eaten," announced the fox proudly. "But tell us, brother wolf, how did you fare? Did you get your pig?"

"My dear friends," moaned the wolf, "let me tell you what happened to me so you will learn from it. I crept through the open door into the dark pigsty and was just about to kill the pig when the wind slammed the door shut. Seeing that the window was too small for me to get out I became very worried, and I looked for another opening to escape.

"While I was running around the wind blew the door open again, but when I rushed out a horrible voice cried, 'Kick the bucket,' and a stream of boiling hot water fell on my back. Oh, how it hurt and how it is still hurting."

"Oh, you poor thing," cried the bear, the fox, and the rabbit. "Is there anything we can do?"

"You can't do anything for me," replied the wolf. "But you can learn from my great misfortune. If ever you go thieving, run as fast as you can if you hear a voice cry, 'Kick the bucket.' "

"Thanks for telling us," said the bear, the rabbit, and the fox. Just then the farmer yelled, "Kick the bucket."

"Run for your life," cried the wolf, and the animals took off like lightning. Smiling from ear to ear, the farmer crawled out from under the trough and took home the honey, the cabbage, and the geese.

The next day he finished the trough and slaughtered the pig. His wife boiled the cabbage, roasted the geese, and made fine honey cakes from the honey. On New Year's Day they invited everybody in the village, including the miser, and they feasted and laughed and laughed and feasted, and afterwards I came and told them a story.

The End

❖

The Three Hundred Iron Rods
A Story About the Values of Honesty and Respect

Long ago, when goods were transported in covered wagons, a wagoner took a load of salt from the city of Salzburg to the city of Nuremberg. After he had sold it he bought three hundred iron rods and loaded them on his wagon. By the time all the transactions had taken place it was night, and he stopped at the trader's inn.

When he arrived the innkeeper handed him a letter and said, "My good man, this letter arrived for you the other day. I hope it is good news." The wagoner opened the letter and read that he had to take a load of goods from the city of Nuremberg to the city of Vienna. He shared the letter's contents with the innkeeper and asked, "Would it be possible to store my three hundred iron rods under your stairway? I will be glad to compensate you for using the space."

"No need for that," replied the innkeeper. "I'll be happy to do a small service for a good customer, and guard them as if they were my own."

Believing the innkeeper, the wagoner left the following day without a worry. He meant to be back within a month, but got delayed. After a fourth of a year had passed the innkeeper said to himself, "I doubt that the wagoner will come back. He probably met his fate somewhere on the highways. I think I'll sell the iron rods, and make some extra money." He found a buyer and sold the rods for a lot of money.

A few weeks later the wagoner returned to the inn and said, "I have come for my rods."

"I must apologize," said the innkeeper. "They are no longer here. I happened to look underneath the stairway the other day, and I found the mice had eaten the rods."

"Is that so?" said the wagoner. "I must confess I would like to see a mouse that can eat iron. But what is gone is gone." He left and spent the night at a friend's house. In the meantime the innkeeper was delighted that he had gotten away with his bad deed. He was like a child who closes his eyes and believes no one can see him.

The following morning the innkeeper's son went out into the street to play. After a while the wagoner drove by with his empty wagon. When he saw the boy he said, "Boy, you remember me, don't you? I have been a guest at your father's inn. Would you like to have a ride in my wagon?"

The boy was delighted. He climbed into the wagon and he and the wagoner rode down the street. At the next street corner the wagoner turned his wagon and went back to his friend's house. When he arrived, he took the boy inside and said, "Son, I must tell you something that will make you sad. Your father is a thief.

"He stole my iron rods, and you must help us to cure him of stealing, or else he will end up on the gallows. Stay here with my friends and be as good as you can be. I promise to come back in eight days and return you to your father."

Because the boy didn't want his father to end up on the gallows, he promised to stay and not run away. Eight days later the wagoner returned to the inn, where he found everyone in black mourning clothes. He asked sympathetically, "Who of your loved ones has departed from this world?"

"My son," wept the innkeeper. "He has disappeared, and we think he is dead. He vanished the day after you came to my house. You didn't see him by any chance?"

The wagoner rubbed his forehead and replied slowly, "Now that you mention it, the day I left I saw a huge bird carrying off a child. Could that have been your son?"

"How dare you to jest," cried the innkeeper angrily. "A bird cannot carry a ten-year-old child away."

The wagoner shrugged his shoulders and replied, "I must say I wondered about that, too. But in a city where mice eat iron, anything can happen."

"Oh my God," cried the innkeeper. "Dearest wagoner, I confess, I sold your iron rods, and I will give you the money. Should you happen to know the whereabouts of my son, return him to me, for God's sake."

While the innkeeper ran for the money, the wagoner went to his friend's house to get the boy. After the boy and his father were reunited the wagoner got up to leave, but just before he opened the door he said, "Being a wagoner, I would have many opportunities to steal, but I know dishonest gain will never last. So why take the risk?"

"I have learned my lesson and I thank you for teaching it to me," said the innkeeper. "I shall have a woodcarver carve those words in the beam above my front entrance, so I will never forget them."

He did, and he became so scrupulously honest that people began to call his inn "The Inn of the Honest Man." If ever you go to the city of Nuremberg, you might want to spend the night there.

The End

❖

The King and
the Broommaker
A Story About the Value of Honesty

One day a kind and caring king invited his friends for dinner. The food was, as usual, good and wholesome, and everybody ate to their heart's content. Only the king didn't seem to have an appetite. After eating a few morsels he put down his fork and said to his guests, "Maybe you can help me. How is it that I own all the forests in this country, and I never collect any revenues from my forest officials?"

Smiling grimly, an old general, who was sitting at the king's left side, took a piece of butter and gave it to the guest on his left side. "Pass it to the king," he said, "and see what happens."

The piece of butter passed through the hands of all the guests, and by the time it reached the king there was hardly anything left. As the king stared at the butter, the old general said, "Your Majesty, had there been more people at this table the butter would have been gone before it reached you. Your money passes through too many hands, and it sticks to some hands more than others. It's the king's job to find out what goes on in his country."

"Timely advice is as lovely as golden apples in a silver basket," replied the king. "Rest assured, I will get to the root of the problem."

The next day the king put on some old clothes and marched off into his country. At times he worked as a woodcutter, at other times he pretended to be a vagrant, and asked for food in some of the forest officials' kitchens. Wherever he went he listened carefully and got a lot of needed information.

One night he came to a poor broommaker's hut. Being very hungry, he asked for a meal. Because the broommaker's wife was not well, the broommaker himself gave him a bowl of thin cabbage soup with not a scrap of meat in it. After the king had eaten, the broommaker said, "No one gets anything for nothing around here. Come and help me to cut some birch branches."

After a long walk they came to a birch grove. "This birch grove belongs to the king," said the broommaker. "Do not cut any branches above the first five growth rings. The birch trees need them for survival."

Wondering what the broommaker would do if he did not obey his order, the king purposely cut some birch branches above the first five growth rings. When the broommaker saw what he had done, he boxed the king's ears and shouted furiously, "Can't you hear, you dolt? I told you this birch grove belongs to the king, and I aim not to cheat him."

Rubbing his sore ears the king asked, "Who would dare to cheat the king?"

"You don't know anything," replied the broommaker bitterly. "Those thieving officials of his are the first ones to grease their palms behind his back."

"Are you sure you are telling me the truth?" asked the king.

"I hear and see it every day, and I hope that one of these days the king will see the light and throw the big thieves into jail right along with the little ones," replied the broommaker. "How can he expect the common folks to be honest when his officials get away with murder?"

After three hours of strenuous work the king and the broommaker came home and found the wife moaning. "Oh my goodness, the child is coming early," cried the broommaker, all upset. "Keep an eye on her. I must run and get the midwife."

He ran off into the night, but by the time he came back with the midwife, the child had been born, and the king was bathing it. After he had dried it the king put the child into the mother's arms and lay down on a wooden bench, hoping to get some rest. But the broommaker pulled him off the bench and said, "A lazy man sleeps soundly but goes hungry. Come and tear some branches so I can tie the brooms."

They worked until the rooster crowed, and after a meager breakfast the king helped the broommaker to carry the brooms to the city. As they entered the gate the king said, "These brooms are well done. I have a hunch that a lot of people would be willing to pay two dollars apiece instead of one."

"Doesn't the law say we can charge only one dollar apiece?" asked the broommaker.

"You are not robbing the king if you sell your brooms for what they are worth," said the king. "I would stay and help you sell them, but I have an errand to run." Before the broommaker could ask more questions the king disappeared into the crowd and rushed back to his palace. There he bade his servants to go out and buy as many brooms as possible and not to haggle about the price.

Soon there was a long line of people trying to buy brooms. "The fellow seems to be right," said the broommaker to himself. "My brooms are in great demand, and I might as well charge two dollars apiece." In no time the brooms were sold, and the broommaker started to walk homeward.

But when he came to the city gate two guards arrested him and brought him before the king. "Who gave you permission to sell brooms at two dollars apiece," thundered the king. "Don't you know that brooms may not be sold for more than one dollar?" The broommaker was very frightened, but trusting the king's righteousness he replied, "Your Majesty, may I tell you what happened?"

"It better be the truth," replied the king, and he listened intently as the broommaker told him about the vagrant, the birth of his child, and the vagrant's advice. When he had finished his tale the king asked, "Would you recognize the rogue who gave you such bad advice if we brought him here?"

"I would," replied the broommaker.

"Wait a minute then," replied the king, and he stepped into an adjoining room. Minutes later the vagrant walked out.

"You rascal," cried the broommaker. "Although you helped my wife birth the child, I will beat you full sore because you got me into real trouble with your stupid advice."

He took off his belt and was just about to hit the king when the vagrant took off his hat, and the broommaker saw that it was the king. He fell on his knees and cried, "Oh dearest king, I am so sorry. Can you forgive me?"

"I have nothing to forgive," laughed the king. "As a matter of fact I am indebted to you. I wish all the people in my kingdom were as honest as you. Take your money, go back to your wife, and when the boy I helped deliver is old enough to be educated, bring him to me and I'll see to it that he gets into a good school."

The broommaker thanked the king and went home with a happy heart. The king, in the meantime, sat down and tried to figure out a way to curb his officials' greed.

The End

Hans and Grete, Nineteen Now

A Drug-Awareness Allegory About the Value of Responsibility and Self-Respect

Not long ago a woman and her husband had twin children. They named the boy Hans after his Swedish grandfather and the girl Grete after her German grandmother. The twins had everything children needed. Their mother took good care of them, and their father was a good provider.

But when Hans and Grete were in their early teens, the father lost his well-paying job. He tried hard to find another one, but the country was in a recession, and jobs were scarce. As the weeks and months passed the father became increasingly embittered, and he began to drink more than he should have.

The mother tried to keep the family going, but her income was small, and paid only for the most necessary things. Soon they had to sell their house and move into an apartment. From then on the parents fought constantly, and driven by despair, the mother joined in on the father's drinking sprees.

Soon the family's home life went from bad to worse, and before long, the twins received blows instead of hugs. One day Hans asked for some money for schoolbooks. Furious that she was unable to give it to him, the mother yelled, "You know I don't have any money. I wish you were gone forever and ever and ever."

That evening Hans said to Grete, "Do you think Mom and Dad would be better off if we left for awhile?"

"I've thought about it," replied Grete. "But where are we to go?"

"I saw a show on homeless kids in a big city," replied Hans. "They seemed to be able to manage. We'll just go away for a few months and see what happens."

"I saw the show, too, and it was horrible," cried Grete. "Those kids led a terrible life. Most of them were on drugs, and the things they did to get money were disgusting. Don't you think there are other ways to seek help?"

"Whom would we ask for help?" asked Hans. "Our teachers? The cops? That would humiliate Mom and Dad, and we would be really in trouble. We don't have to do the things those kids do. We can find a place to sleep and scrounge around for food, and we'll be all right."

"I'll think about it," replied Grete. A few days later, their parents had another one of those stormy scenes. And that night, while their parents were sleeping, the twins put a few necessities into their old duffel bags and left.

A bus took them to a big ugly city. Luck was with them. In return for a few hours of sorting used car parts, the owner of a run-down salvage lot allowed them to live in an old van and use the loo [toilet]. Rummaging for food in garbage cans was more difficult.

Not only did they have to dodge the police for fear that they would put them into a home for runaway teens, they also had to stay out of the way of criminals, who were prowling the city streets.

Hans and Grete learned to walk in the shadows of buildings and disappear into alleys; they learned how it felt to be hungry and terrified.

Weeks passed, and the twins began to talk about calling their parents, collect, to see if they would want them to come home. But before they could do it, calamity struck. One day, while searching for food, Hans and Grete took a wrong turn and lost their way.

Evening came, and as they hurried through unfamiliar streets, anxious to find a safe place to sleep, Hans noticed that a car was following them. As it drew nearer the driver rolled down his window and yelled, "You wanna ride?"

Sure that he meant trouble, the twins walked to the other side of the street, as if they knew where they were going. The driver watched them for a few minutes and drove off.

Hoping that they had gotten rid of him, Hans and Grete turned into a quiet side street, when suddenly they saw the same car again. It was parked in the shadow of a huge tree with the night prowler still in it.

By now the twins were terrified. Not only were they all alone, but the street was as dark and empty as a grave. Not a single light was shining, and all the houses were boarded up.

"Let's go back to the main street," whispered Hans. They started to run, but the car came roaring after them. It was like a cat-and-mouse game, and the cat almost got them. But suddenly a bus came around the corner, filling the dark street with its blinding light.

The twins rushed to the bus stop and waved, and when the old vehicle stopped they scampered on board. But the bus driver took one look at them and snarled, "You got some money?"

"No," sputtered Hans, all embarrassed. "We didn't plan to ride a bus. We only came to the bus stop because a guy was following us, and we were scared."

"I don't care if someone is following you or not," said the bus driver. "You pay and I give you a ride. You don't pay and you get off. This is not a charity bus."

"Couldn't you just take us to the next main street?" begged Grete.

"Out!" shouted the bus driver. "I wasn't hired to drive juvenile delinquents around the city. Get out or I throw you out."

Close to tears, the twins picked up their duffel bags and were just about to climb down the steps when a woman passenger got up from her seat and said, "Hold it, bus driver. You can't chase those kids out into the night. They were telling the truth. I saw the car they were speaking of, and you saw it, too. Do you want to have two dead kids on your conscience?"

"Conscience, schmonscience," screamed the bus driver, now thoroughly enraged. "You stay out of this, lady, unless you want to pay their fare. If I say they leave the bus, they will leave the bus. I have been cheated too often."

"Cool it," replied the woman. "I am going to pay."

"Put your money where your mouth is," snapped the bus driver. "Where to?"

"Unheil Street," replied the lady, and she put the necessary coins into the box.

"Thanks for saving our lives," said Hans as he and Grete followed her to the back of the bus. "Can you give us your address? We'll send you the money as soon as we get home."

"Don't fib, honey," laughed the woman. "Everyone can see that you two don't have a home. You can stay the night with me, and you better take my offer. That ape of a bus driver might spot a cop and turn you in."

"Can he do that?" stuttered Grete.

"Of course he can," replied the woman. "But don't worry. I am going to take care of you."

And care for them she did, but had Hans and Grete known what was in store for them they would have jumped off the bus at the next stop and found a police officer. They were right to be afraid of the night prowler. But they were wrong to be afraid of the police: It was that fear that sent them falling from the frying pan into a big fire.

The twins had their first misgivings when they arrived at the woman's house. It was a huge, sinister-looking old place, surrounded by a big stone wall. No lights could be seen from the street, and when they got inside the woman locked the heavy oak door with three different keys.

Then she took the twins into a shabby-looking kitchen, and after she handed them a bag of potato chips and some cold ham, she said, "It's time we get acquainted. What are your names?"

"My name is Hans," replied Hans, "and my sister's name is Grete."

"Hansel and Gretel," cackled the woman. "You must be kidding. Are those your real names?"

"Not Hansel and Gretel. Our names are Hans and Grete," explained Grete, annoyed. Although she was used to being teased about her name, it bugged her each time it happened.

"Don't get your nose out of joint," snickered the woman. "It's just so funny. My trade name is Crack-Witch. Ha, ha, ha. Hansel and Gretel and Crack-Witch. This is too good to be true."

"What are you talking about?" cried Grete, horrified. "Are you a drug dealer?"

"You catch on quick," laughed Crack-Witch. "And now I will tell you the story of 'Hansel and Gretel' the way it happens n-o-w. It is a very funny story.

"One day two children by the name of Hans and Grete ran away from home. When they came to a big city they were caught by a woman named Crack-Witch. 'You will have to join all the children I have captured, and deliver my wares to my customers,' cackled Crack-Witch.

"'Tomorrow I will teach you what to do, and if you know what is good for you, you'll follow the rules, or you will disappear without a trace.' And they did, and Crack-Witch lived happily ever after."

The next day Hans and Grete met the other children and they became a part of the world of drugs with all of its horror, deceit, despair, fear, and hopelessness.

Because Crack-Witch allowed her helpers to use crack Hans soon joined the rest of the kids and got hooked, but Grete did not. Her parents' addiction had taught her an indelible lesson. At night, when Hans and the rest of the kids got high, Grete busied herself in the house. Not wanting to be locked up in her room with nothing to do but worry, she began to clean the old kitchen, which no one used any longer.

It took her a long time to scrub the kitchen furniture, and finally there was only one cupboard left. Its contents were nothing special. Stacks of old newspapers. At least twenty-five beer bottles. An old tennis ball, and underneath some filthy old dish towels a bunch of rusty keys.

Grete threw everything into a plastic bag. It didn't occur to her until late that night that the keys might be the tools to her and Hans's escape. The following evening, after a harrowing day, she managed to smuggle the keys into her room.

That night, after Crack-Witch had locked up everyone and gone into her room, Grete crept to her door and tried out the keys. When she found the key that fit her lock, she knew she had to find a way to escape, although she was well aware of what would happen to her and Hans if she failed.

She set her mind to work, and a few nights later she let herself out of her room. She sneaked downstairs into the basement and unscrewed all the fuses. Leaving the basement door open, she hid behind a coatrack on which hung old clothes. Then she took the tennis ball and threw it at the big hall window.

The noise of the shattering glass woke up Crack-Witch, but when she flipped on the light switch the lights did not go on. Sure that thieves had entered her house she grabbed a powerful flashlight and her gun and rushed to the landing, yelling at the top of her voice, "Hands up or I'll blow you to pieces."

When no one stirred she crept cautiously downstairs and pointed her light into the living room, the dining room, and the kitchen. Finding these rooms empty she walked into the back hallway and discovered the open basement door. Sure that the thieves had fled to the basement she stepped on the top step and flooded the basement stairs with light, screaming, "Come out or I'll...."

Before she could say, "shoot," Grete dashed forward, pushed her down the basement steps and locked the door behind her. Then she rushed to the evil woman's room and called the police.

The next day the newspapers were filled with the gruesome details of Crack-Witch's crimes, how she had bullied and terrorized scores of teens into submission, and how many of her victims had disappeared without a trace.

There also appeared a list of all the treasures she had amassed. The police found a burglar-proof vault that contained thousands of dollars in cash, ten passports from ten different countries, four suitcases packed with the finest clothes, and a fifth suitcase with wigs of all shapes and colors for disguise if ever she had to leave in a hurry. Well, she left the house, but not in a hurry and not to go to another country.

When Grete pushed her, Crack-Witch lost her balance and tumbled down the basement steps. Falling on a heap of old copper pipes she hit her head and was unconscious until the police found her. And so ended her life of crime.

And what happened to the children? Grete went back to her parents, who had pulled their lives together. Hans and the rest of the boys and girls went to a drug rehabilitation center and eventually became drug free.

All was well at the end, but the price the twins paid was too high.

The End

Bird Baby Don't Fly

A Story About the Values of Respect and Responsibility

"GUN ON SCHOOL GROUND KILLS INNOCENT BYSTANDER," screamed the Tuesday headline. The tragedy happened at a school where I tell stories on Fridays. "Did you hear about the fight?" shouted the students when I arrived. "There is going to be another one this afternoon." All of them were nervous and excited. Some were looking forward to the fight, and others were not. Fortunately there was no fight. Several police cars were patrolling the streets when I left, and the day ended peacefully.

But there was no peace in my heart. From what I heard, I knew I had to find a story that dealt with the role of the cheering bystanders. It had to be simple, nonpreaching, and help the students to become aware of the brutal finality of death. I ended up writing "Bird Baby Don't Fly."

The following week I divided the students into two groups, and asked them to participate in the telling of "Bird Baby Don't Fly." Their task was to play Mother Bird's friends. Since I found out from experience that invitations to discuss stories usually evoked silence, I asked my students afterwards to write anonymous letters to the characters in the story.

The purpose of the letter-writing activity was to give them an opportunity to write about their feelings and anxieties about fighting without the fear of ridicule. It did, and I hope the story of Bird Baby will help them to make the right choices if ever they should be in a similar situation again.

One year Bird Mother hatched out three children. She fed them and kept them clean, and when she saw that they were strong enough to fly she began to give them flying lessons. The two older ones quickly overcame their fear of leaving the nest. After a few awkward starts they flew happily about and rejoiced in their newly found freedom. Only little Yukpa, Bird Mother's youngest child, was still teeter-tottering on the rim of the nest, too scared to fly off.

"Fly, little Yukpa, fly," coaxed Bird Mother, and she demonstrated over and over again how it was done. Finally, little Yukpa hopped off the rim of the nest and floated to the forest ground. "Good, good," chirped Bird Mother, and she sang proudly,

Yukpa, my brave little Yukpa,
You flew out of your nest.
You learned to flap your sturdy wings,
And the wind will do the rest.

Proud of his mother's praise, little Yukpa started to flap his wings in order to fly back to the nest when suddenly he saw two big animals coming his way. Terrified by their size he cried, "Mother dear, will those animals hurt me?"

"Look at them and remember that they are stags," replied Bird Mother. "I think their names are Wah-bit and Wadjebi, and I know they don't harm birds."

"Are you sure?" twittered little Yukpa nervously.

"I am sure," replied Bird Mother. "Now fly back to the nest and don't worry about every strange animal you see. I am the strongest bird in the forest, and I can and will protect you."

Once again little Yukpa began to flap his wings. Very likely he would have made it back to the nest were it not for Wah-bit and Wadjebi. Thinking it extremely funny that tiny Bird Mother claimed to be the biggest and strongest bird in the forest, they came closer and teased,

> Bird baby don't fly,
> Your mother told you a lie.
> Do not believe what you heard,
> She's nothing but a weak, old bird.

"Hold your tongues and leave us alone," chirped Bird Mother angrily. "You should know that for my children I have to be the strongest bird in the forest."

But Wadjebi and Wah-bit would not leave. They kept on chanting,

> Bird baby don't fly,
> Your mother told you a lie.
> Do not believe what you heard,
> She's nothing but a weak, old bird.

"Mamma," cried little Yukpa, "do you hear what they are saying?"

"Pay no attention," scolded Bird Mother, and she repeated her song of praise.

> Yukpa, my brave little Yukpa,
> Please fly back to your nest.
> You know how to flap your sturdy wings,
> And the wind will do the rest.

But her baby wouldn't fly. Although the stags left after awhile, they had stolen Yukpa's confidence in his mother, and he remained sitting on the forest ground, too scared to move.

The day passed slowly. The sun went down in the west, and the sky turned dark. The forest grew quiet. Only the shrill voice of Bird Mother penetrated the stillness of the night.

"Yukpa, my brave little Yukpa," on and on and on she cried, begging her little son to fly back to the nest, but it was to no avail. A few hours later a huge nighthawk swooped down from a tree and carried little Yukpa away.

Overcome by grief, Bird Mother slept for the rest of the night, but as soon as the sun came up she flew to her bird friends and told them what had happened. "I blame Wah-bit and Wadjebi for my Yukpa's death," she cried, "and I will punish them."

"What can a small bird like you do to punish two big stags?" asked the birds.

"If I come up with a plan will you help me?" asked Bird Mother. The birds nodded their heads, and Bird Mother flew back to her nest to think.

Early the next morning, while Wah-bit was drinking water by the lake, Bird Mother flew up to him and chirped, "Why, Wah-bit, you look mighty strong to me. I can't understand why your brother boasts that he is stronger than you."

"Wadjebi claims to be stronger than me?" asked Wah-bit, who did not remember Bird Mother.

"That's what I've heard," replied Bird Mother. "I saw him grazing at the big clearing. Why don't you go and teach him not to tell lies."

"I will," shouted Wah-bit angrily, and he rushed into the forest. Meanwhile Bird Mother flew ahead of him to Wadjebi and said, "Wadjebi, is it true that your brother Wah-bit would defeat you if the two of you got into a fight?"

Wadjebi did not remember Bird Mother either, and he replied furiously, "Who says things like that?"

"Wah-bit does," replied Bird Mother. "He is coming this way. Why don't you teach him not to tell lies."

"I certainly will," cried Wadjebi, and he ran to meet his brother.

Pleased that her plan was working, Bird Mother flew back to her friends and said, "Wadjebi and Wah-bit will fight to find out who is the stronger one. Some of you must cheer for Wah-bit, some of you must cheer for Wadjebi, and you must not stop cheering until I tell you to."

The birds followed Bird Mother to the clearing and found Wah-bit and Wadjebi shouting at each other. "How dare you go around claiming that you are stronger than me?" bellowed Wah-bit.

"How dare you brag that you would beat me in a fight?" roared Wadjebi.

"Stop arguing and show us which of you is the stronger one," shrieked Bird Mother, and that was all that was needed to start the fight between the two brothers. They began to ram into each other. Dash, crash. Dash, crash.

Meanwhile, just as they had been told, one half of the assembled forest birds took Wah-bit's side and cheered,

Wah-bit, Wah-bit, do it right,
Wah-bit, you will win this fight.

while the other half cheered for Wadjebi,

Wadjebi, Wadjebi, do it right,
Wadjebi, you will win this fight.

Soon the forest was filled with a terrible din. Egged on by the cheering of the birds, the two stags fought like they had never fought before. They crashed into each other until sweat began to pour from their bodies and foam came from their nostrils. Dash, crash. Dash, crash. Dash, crash.

After a while all the bones in their bodies began to ache, and both were ready to stop fighting. But neither was willing to admit defeat as long as the birds were still cheering,

Wadjebi, Wadjebi, do it right.
Wah-bit, you will win this fight.

They fought all morning. They fought through the hot noon hour. They fought all afternoon. Dash, crash. Dash, crash. On and on and on. Dash, crash. Dash, crash, until suddenly in the late afternoon the birds heard one more loud crash, and then there was silence.

They stopped cheering and looked. What was going on? Why were Wah-bit and Wadjebi no longer fighting? Why were they standing so still? Bird Mother was the first to realize what had happened. "Look, look," she cried. "Wah-bit and Wadjebi's antlers are locked."

"Their antlers are locked. Wah-bit's and Wadjebi's antlers are locked," cried the horrified birds, and they watched silently as Wah-bit and Wadjebi tucked and pulled, and pulled and tucked, trying to disengage from each other.

But all their efforts were in vain. They were stuck. They couldn't bend to eat grass. They couldn't walk to the lake to drink water. They couldn't lie down to rest. All they could do was to stare into each other's eyes and wait for death to free them from their agony.

The forest birds stayed for a while, but eventually they grew hungry and flew away. Soon after, their silent cousins, the vultures, arrived. They settled quietly on the branches of the surrounding trees, waiting for Wah-bit and Wadjebi to die so they could do their grizzly job.

Bird baby don't fly,
Your mother told you a lie.
Do not believe what you heard,
She's nothing but a weak, old bird.

It all started with a few heedless words, but isn't it amazing how a few words or a thoughtless deed can cause so much damage?

The End

❖

The Boy Who Called the King a Fool

A Story About the Value of Responsibility

Long ago the king of Laquay invited the king of Sinsabarra to hunt in his forests. The hunt was a great success. Hundreds of forest animals were killed, and when evening came all the hunters felt good about their day's work. The banquet following the hunt was even better. There was enough food to feed an army and enough vodka to fill a river.

Unfortunately the two oldest sons of the kings drank too much vodka and got into a terrible fight. Before anyone could stop them they challenged one another to a duel and shot each other to death.

When the king of Laquay saw his dead son lying on the ground he shook his fist at the king of Sinsabarra and shouted, "Your son shot mine, and for that you shall suffer. I hereby declare war on you and your accursed nation."

The king of Sinsabarra looked mournfully at his dead son and replied, "My son would have never raised his weapon against anyone unless he was mortally insulted. I shall see to it that his death is avenged."

Both kings began to prepare for war, and on the day the Laquayen soldiers left for the battlefields their king addressed them and said, "My fellow Laquayens, you are the bravest and best trained soldiers in the world." The soldiers cheered, and the king continued, "My son was killed, and it is your sacred duty to avenge his death. If you fight those Sansabarras without mercy, victory will be your gain, and you will receive your just rewards."

Once again the soldiers cheered, but their cheering was interrupted by a woman who had come to say good-bye to her only son. She stepped up to the king and asked, "And what will happen if our soldiers are not victorious?"

For a moment the king was speechless, but then his face turned purple and he thundered, "If those soldiers don't win this battle, they'll be sent to the death camps of Orreply."

Everyone was stunned. What was the king talking about? Criminals were sent to the death camps of Orreply, not soldiers. But no one had the courage to ask for an explanation, and then the drummer boy began to beat his drum—Barr-romm, bomm, bomm. Barr-romm, bomm, bomm. Follow the call of the drum, bomm, bomm—the soldiers followed obediently.

During the first hours of the day the soldiers felt good. They talked about the battles they had won and the valiant deeds they had done. But as the day passed they began to worry about the king's words. Did he really mean that he was going to send them to the death camps of Orreply if they didn't win this battle?

"We had better try our best to win this battle," said one of the sergeants. "A king's fury is like that of a roaring lion. To rouse his anger is to risk your life." The others nodded soberly. Only one shrugged his shoulders and said, "We can't worry about the king's anger. It's our job to risk our lives, and should we end up in Orreply it can't be worse than war."

"Maybe that's the way to look at it," replied some of the others, and they rode on silently, each occupied with his own thoughts. After a while they passed a farmhouse. A ragged-looking boy, who was busy sweeping the yard, stopped his work and stared at their beautiful red-and-gold uniforms.

All of a sudden he threw down his broom and ran after them. The soldiers tried to send him back to his farm, but he would not listen. "Please take me with you," he shouted. "I want to come with you." After a while the army cook gave in and allowed him to ride on one of the provision carts.

Evening came and the boy helped the soldiers set up camp and cook their meals. As they sat around the fire and ate, the conversation returned to the king's words. "I fought many wars, and by now I know that all of them were useless," said a veteran soldier, "but this one is the craziest one of all. It doesn't make sense to me that hundreds of men will have to die because two drunken fools killed each other."

"Kings should have to fight their own wars," muttered one of the younger soldiers, and he spat into the fire. Their conversation stopped when a corporal joined them and said, "I heard you picked up a boy on the way. Our drummer boy got sick, and I must find someone to take his place."

"I'll take his place," cried the boy eagerly. "I'll learn how to beat the drum."

"Good for you," replied the corporal, "but listen well, a lot depends on you. A drum is the heartbeat of a battle. It gives the soldiers direction to either advance or to retreat, and the one who beats it must never lose heart and stop."

"I'll beat that drum like no one ever beat it before," promised the boy, and he went with the corporal to his tent and learned to beat the battle rhythms of the Laquayen army.

Barr-romm, bomm, bomm. Barr-romm, bomm, bomm. Follow the call of the drum, bomm, bomm.

The following day they rode on, and no one was prouder than the new drummer boy. All day long he practiced beating the drum.

Barr-romm, bomm, bomm. Barr-romm, bomm, bomm. By evening they reached the battlefield, and when morning came they met the enemy.

Barr-romm, bomm, bomm. Barr-romm, bomm, bomm. Follow the call of the drum, bomm, bomm, sang the drum, and the soldiers on both sides rushed toward each other and began to shoot. Within minutes the air was filled with the screaming of wounded men and horses, and the boy, who had never seen anything like it, watched in horror as people mowed each other down like wheat stalks.

It was so awful that he would have liked to run, but he remembered his promise and kept on beating his drum:

Barr-romm, bomm, bomm. Barr-romm, bomm, bomm. Follow the call of the drum, bomm, bomm. Over and over and over. Barr-romm, bomm, bomm, until one of the bullets came his way and knocked him down.

But the boy didn't stay down for long. When he was able to sit up and realized that only his right arm was wounded, he wrapped his neckerchief around the wound and continued to beat the drum with his left hand.

Barr-romm, bomm, bomm. Barr-romm, bomm, bomm. Follow the call of the drum, bomm, bomm. But after a while the pain set in, and even though he tried valiantly to keep on drumming he fainted.

When he awoke he found himself lying in a shallow ditch. His arm was throbbing with pain, and he was terribly thirsty. Pulling all his strength together he managed to creep out of the ditch and look around. What he saw made his blood turn to ice. The battlefield had been turned into a graveyard. Not a single soldier, not a single horse was stirring. All of them were dead.

In spite of his pain the boy got up on his feet and staggered to the nearby river. But when he bent down to drink the water he saw that it was red from the soldiers' blood. A feeling of horror swept over him, and suddenly he remembered the veteran soldier's words: "Hundreds of men will have to die because two drunken fools killed each other."

A thousand men had died, but perhaps it was not the fault of the two drunken fools who had killed each other. It was the fault of the two kings who had declared war. Someone has to tell the king what he has done, thought the boy. Stumbling over and around the dead bodies the boy reached the road that led to the king's city.

As he tottered along, a horseman came his way. He stopped and shouted, "Hey boy, are you coming from the battlefield?" The boy nodded. "What happened?" cried the horseman.

"They are all dead," replied the boy.

"Al-l-l dead?" stammered the horseman.

"Each and every one," said the boy. "And I am on my way to tell the king."

"Don't go!" cried the horseman. "Don't you know the king will send you to the death camp of Orreply if you bring him bad news."

"I know that," replied the boy, "but I must go anyway. I must go and tell the king that no one ever wins a war. Maybe he won't do it again."

"Don't count on it," sighed the horseman. "Don't you know power corrupts? Once folks are up on the top they think they are God, but if you insist on going let me give you my horse. Otherwise you won't make it."

He helped the boy to climb on the horse's back, and the boy rode to the city. But the time he entered the gate he was so exhausted that those who saw him thought he would fall off his horse at any moment. But when he reached the castle he sat up straight and began to beat his drum. Barr-romm, bomm, bomm. Barr-romm, bomm, bomm. Follow the call of the drum, bomm, bomm.

The minute the king heard the drum he came out of his castle to greet his soldiers. When he saw no one but the bloodstained drummer boy, surrounded by a group of anxious-looking women and children, he turned pale and cried, "Are you coming from the battlefield?"

"Yes," said the boy.

"Tell me what happened," cried the king.

"I beat a dead skin, and it called the living to die." replied the boy.

"I didn't ask you to tell me what you did. I asked you to tell me what you saw," shouted the king.

"I saw precious mixed with precious, but it has no value," replied the boy.

"Don't talk to me in riddles," screeched the king. "I order you to tell me what happened."

"Two fools declared war, and a thousand died because of two," whispered the boy with his last ounce of strength. Then he let go of his drum and fell off his horse and died.

"My army lost the battle," stuttered the king, and he staggered toward his castle. But he never got there. A young woman picked up the drum and began to beat it. And as she beat it she sobbed:

Two fools declared war,
And a thousand had to die.
Come on, foolish king, come and bury the dead,
While we come along and cry.

"No," shouted the king, "I don't want to bury a thousand dead people."

"Who else shall bury them?" cried the women and children, and they dragged him to the battlefield. But when the king saw all the dead he fainted, and when he came to he wasn't fit to bury anyone. He had lost his mind.

Until the day he died, the king walked along the highways of his country, muttering, "Two fools declared war, and a thousand had to die." At first the people pointed him out to their children, saying, "Look, there goes the foolish king who started a war that killed a thousand men." But in time they forgot the war, forgot the dead, forgot that he had been their king, and just called him "The Fool."

The End

A Perjurer Is a Liar
A Story About the Values of Truthfulness and Responsibility

A woodcarver by the name of Zachariah had the good luck to sell a beautiful statue for a hundred silver dollars. Because this didn't happen too often, he and his wife, Resi, invited their neighbors to celebrate. At the end of the party the hosts and the guests linked arms and danced around the table singing happily:

Woodcarvers make statues out of wood,
Ree-dee, rall-lalla, ree-dee-rall-lalla,
And folks will buy them, if they're good.
Ree-dee, rall-lalla, rall-lalla-la.

Everyone but their next-door neighbors Karrel and Britt was happy for them. When they went home that night Karrel said, "A hundred silver dollars for a measly statue. People are crazy to spend that much money on useless stuff."

"I wish I had the hundred silver dollars," said Britt enviously.

"Maybe we could find a way to get them," said Karrel.

"How would you do that?" asked Britt.

"I'll think of a way," said Karrel, and he began to make plans to cheat his neighbors out of their money. A few days later Britt rubbed beet juice all over her face, and went to bed, moaning so loudly that the neighbors came running. But Karrel came to the door and waved them away.

"Don't come inside. Britt is desperately ill, and it might be catching. Just look through the bedroom window and tell me, could it be the same disease her grandmother had? About ten years ago she too turned bright red one day, and a week later she was dead."

The neighbors peeked through the window, and seeing Britt's bright red face, they ran to their houses and started to boil vinegar water to clean the air. Only Resi asked if she could be of any help, but Karrel would not have her do a thing. In the meantime Britt carried on, and moaned and moaned and moaned.

"Is she going to die?" asked Zachariah's daughter Rieva.

"We don't know," replied her mother. "Let's pray for her."

They began to pray, but their prayers were interrupted by a loud knock. Zachariah went to the door, and there stood Karrel.

"Zachariah, I just remembered a deaf woman from my old village. They say she can cure people with deadly diseases. But because there is always the risk that she will catch the disease herself, her family asks for a lot of money in advance. And so, God help me, I don't have the money."

"Take my hundred silver dollars," said Zachariah, and he went into the bedroom and got his moneybag.

"I'll pay it back as soon as I can," cried Karrel, and he ran back to his house.

"Are you sure Karrel will pay it back?" asked Rieva, who didn't like Karrel and Britt.

"Shush," said her mother. "He will as soon as he can."

In the meantime Karrel went to his old village, returning with an old, deaf aunt who did not know much about sickness. She did Britt's housework, however, and when Britt decided to be well again, she returned to her village.

Three months passed, and Zachariah and Resi began to wonder about their money. They could have used it, but they made do. Six months passed, and at the end of the seventh month Zachariah said to Karrel, "Karrel, I have an order for several wooden statues, and I need my hundred silver dollars to purchase wood."

"But I gave it back to you," said Karrel, astonished.

"Not that I remember," replied Zachariah. "I am sure you meant to give it back, but you haven't yet."

"I can't believe what you are saying," cried Karrel. "I really thank you for lending us the money, but we paid it back months ago."

"Karrel," replied Zachariah quietly, "because Britt was so ill, we thought you needed time to come up with the money. But I swear you haven't paid it back."

"And I swear I gave it back," shouted Karrel, now thoroughly enraged. "Get out of here, you liar. I wish you had never given me the money."

No one had ever called Zachariah a liar, and it was the insult more than the loss of money that made him go to the judge.

The judge agreed to hear the case, and both men had to appear in court. The night before the hearing Rieva asked, "What happens if Karrel lies to the judge?"

"If Karrel lies to the judge he becomes a perjurer," replied Zachariah. "And if he is found out he goes to jail."

"Why do they call him a perjurer and not just a liar?" asked Rieva.

"A perjurer doesn't only lie to people, he also lies to God," explained her father. The next day Zachariah and Karrel presented their case to the judge.

"I can't determine which one of you is telling the truth by just listening to you," said the judge. "Both of you must take the oath." Zachariah, dressed in a simple suit, put his left hand on the Bible and, raising his right hand, he swore that he was telling the truth and nothing but the truth.

Next Karrel, wearing a new suit and carrying a heavy walking stick, walked up to the bench. Realizing that he needed both hands to take this oath, he handed the walking stick to Zachariah and said, "Hold it for a minute."

His action took Zachariah by surprise. But he felt it was beneath his dignity to refuse and he held the stick while Karrel swore that he had given the money back.

Because both men had sworn on the Bible the judge dismissed their case.

As the men walked out of the courthouse Karrel said, "Zachariah, next time you accuse me of stealing your money I'll sue you for slander." Zachariah did not reply, but Rieva, who was waiting with her mother on the courthouse steps, cried, "I saw Dad give the money to you, and I know you never gave it back."

"Hush your mouth, you little brat," hissed Karrel. "This is none of your business."

"Oh yes it is," cried Rieva. "My Dad said a perjurer is a liar who lies to God and people. Aren't you scared to be a perjurer?"

"I'll teach you to call me a perjurer," cried Karrel furiously, and he lifted his walking stick and tried to hit Rieva.

"Don't you dare hit my daughter," yelled Zachariah, and he yanked the walking stick out of Karrel's hand.

"Give me back my walking stick," bellowed Karrel, and he took hold of the stick with both hands and tugged as hard as he could. Suddenly the stick snapped in two, and silver dollars spilled all over the place.

The judge, who had heard their loud voices through the open door, came running outside and picked up the two pieces of the stick. "Good grief," cried he, "This stick is hollow. The scoundrel put the silver dollars in a hollow walking stick, handed it to his opponent, and swore he had given it back. Now I've seen everything."

While two guards led Karrel to jail, Rieva helped Zachariah and Resi pick up the silver dollars. The following day Zachariah bought a piece of wood and cut out a relief depicting the story. Underneath he carved the words, "Thou shall not bear false witness against thy neighbor."

The End

The Bridge Across the Fire

A Story About the Value of Compassion

In the city of Damascus lived long ago a merchant by the name of Abdul. He was an excellent trader, but he led an evil life. One day Abdul died and went to heaven. He saw the Lord Allah in all his glory but found that between him and the Lord Allah was a deep chasm filled with fire.

"Recite your good deeds, and they will build a bridge across the fire," said the Lord Allah. Abdul began to recite his good deeds, but they were so few that his bridge was no wider than a finger.

Realizing that he could not cross the chasm on a bridge as narrow as that, Abdul suddenly understood that hell meant separation from the Lord Allah throughout eternity. An immense feeling of sorrow swept over him, and he cried, "Oh, Lord Allah, have mercy on me," but he received no answer.

Soon after another man arrived. When his bridge turned out to be no wider than two fingers he began to weep and wail. Seeing his despair, Abdul said, "There is no need for both of us to suffer eternal separation from the Lord Allah. Take my good deeds. They will widen your bridge enough so you can cross the chasm."

Hardly had he said those words when the Lord Allah said, "Abdul, you have shown compassion, and therefore you too may use the bridge."

Full of joy, Abdul crossed the bridge and is now praising the mercy of Allah forever and ever.

The End

Hehheh and the Honey Cakes
A Story About the Values of Humanity and Compassion

On a cold December day Hehheh walked into the town of Nebelregen. Tired from tramping through the snow Hehheh sat down on the steps that led up to the first councilman's house. Suddenly he smelled the smell of honey cakes. Christmas is near, thought Hehheh happily, and he got up and knocked gently at the door.

The councilman's fourteen-year-old-maid, Stina, came to answer the door. Stina knew Hehheh well, and she loved him dearly. "Why, Stina," said Hehheh cheerfully, "I didn't know you were working here. I smelled the smell of honey cakes. Can your mistress spare one for me?"

"Oh, no," whispered Stina. "My mistress wouldn't share a honey cake with St. Peter if he asked for it. But she just stepped out of the kitchen, and while she is gone I'll get you one." Before Hehheh could stop her, Stina scurried into the kitchen, and soon she came back with a honey cake. Putting it in Hehheh's pocket she whispered, "They are delicious. I tasted a crumb. Enjoy it, but don't come back here. My mistress would bite your head off."

"Some rich people are poor, and some poor people have great wealth," mumbled Hehheh as he walked down the steps. But he didn't leave. Instead, he stepped behind an old pine tree with low hanging branches. From there he could look into the kitchen window and see Stina, who had returned to the kitchen and was kneading a ball of dough.

Just as she was about to put the dough on the baking sheet and roll it flat the councilman's wife stormed into the kitchen. She slapped poor Stina's cheeks as hard as she could and screamed, "I happened to look out of the upstairs window and saw you giving one of my freshly baked honey cakes to Hehheh. How dare you give one of my precious honey cakes to that beggar? Get away from the table and go to the corner and polish the master's shoes. I'll finish the honey cakes myself."

Grabbing the ball of dough she slapped it on the baking sheet, but when she tried to roll it out with the rolling pin the dough remained uneven. Thick in the middle, thin on the sides. Thin in the middle, thick on the sides. After a lot of rolling the mistress gave up and slammed the baking sheet into the oven.

Now it takes about twenty minutes of high heat to bake honey cakes, but only ten minutes had gone by when the kitchen was filled with a burning stench. All upset, the mistress tore the oven door open and found that all of her honey cakes had burned. With a face as sour as a pickle she threw the burned cakes into the slop bucket and carried it out on the back porch.

When she came back she floured her hands and tried to lift the remaining dough out of the bowl. But it stuck to the bottom like glue. "What in the world is going on?" cried the infuriated woman. "My first batch of cakes turned out perfectly. Stina, you stupid goose, don't just sit there and stare. Bring me some extra flour from the flour bin. This dough is too soft."

Stina ran to the pantry and returned with more flour. The mistress added a handful of flour to the dough, but the dough stayed as gooey as grilled cheese, and wouldn't come out. She added more and more flour, and when she finally was able to lift the dough out of the bowl it was so brittle and dry that it was nearly impossible to roll out.

By now the mistress was so mad she could have picked a fight with a bear. She pounded the dough on the sheet and pushed it in the oven. She might as well have spared herself the trouble. This time the honey cakes didn't burn, but by the time they came out of the oven they were so hard she could have used them to knock a hole into her head.

After the second batch of honey cakes landed in the slop bucket Hehheh left. He walked leisurely to the apothecary's house and visited for quite a while with his wife and children. Afterward he went to Stina's home. By the time he arrived it was evening, and Stina's parents and their four younger children invited him for supper.

After they had eaten their thick barley soup Hehheh reached into his pocket and took out the honey cake Stina had given to him. He put it on the table, and then he pulled out another one, and another one, and another one. When the whole table was covered with perfect honey cakes, Hehheh chuckled and said, "Help yourself."

None of the family had ever eaten honey cakes like these. They munched them and crunched them until they could not eat another bite. After a while Stina's mother asked, "Hehheh, where did you get those wonderful honey cakes?" Before Hehheh could answer the door flew open and Stina came running inside. Her face was red and swollen, and her eyes were filled with tears. Without being aware of Hehheh, Stina rushed into her mother's arms and cried, "Oh Mamma, today was the worst day I ever lived through. We were baking honey cakes and I gave one to Hehheh...."

"Shh," interrupted Hehheh, and before Stina could say another word, he put a honey cake into her mouth.

"Hehheh," asked Stina, "is this a dream?" Hehheh didn't answer Stina's question. Instead he said "I talked to the apothecary's wife. Her new baby is due within a month. She needs someone to keep an eye on her older children. I know her to be a fine woman. How would you like to work for her?"

"I would do anything if I wouldn't have to go back to the councilman's house," cried Stina.

"She is expecting you as soon as you are ready," said Hehheh, and he said good night and left. Early the next morning Stina went to the councilman's house and gave notice.

"Christmas is coming, and there is a lot of work to do," screamed the councilman's wife. "If you leave me now, I'll tell everyone what a lazy, good-for-nothing wench you are, and no one else will hire you."

"A story sounds true until someone tells the other side and sets the record straight," said a familiar voice. It was Hehheh's. He had slipped into the house and was standing by the kitchen door.

"Get out of here, you miserable imp," shrieked the councilman's wife, and she lifted her arm to strike Hehheh. Suddenly Hehheh's eyes began to flash like lightning, and he thundered, "Your own soul is nourished when you are kind; it is destroyed when you are cruel."

Slowly the angry woman's arm fell to her side. She sat down on a chair and stared at Hehheh as if she had never seen him before. Hehheh put his arm around Stina's shoulder and turned to go. Just before he left he reached into his pocket and handed the councilman's wife a honey cake. As the door closed behind Hehheh and Stina, the councilman's wife put it into her mouth and ate it.

What it did to her I don't know, but afterwards she got up and made a new batch of honey cakes, which turned out perfectly. On Christmas Eve day Hehheh happened to pass by her house. The minute the councilman's wife saw him she rushed outside and cried, "Hehheh, I would be honored if you came and had some tea and honey cakes with me. I know you like to eat them."

Hehheh was glad to come, and when he had eaten his fill he chuckled and said, "You surely make the best honey cakes."

"Wait," said the councilman's wife, and she ran into the kitchen. When she came back she handed Hehheh a big bag filled with honey cakes.

"Keep them for me until I come back tonight," said Hehheh. "You and I have a job to do." That evening he came back, and he and the councilman's wife sneaked through the streets of Nebelregen and left a delicious honey cake at the doorstep of every child in town.

When the children found the honey cakes on Christmas morning they danced in the streets and sang,

Santa Claus, Santa Claus,
Brought honey cakes to our house.
Thank you, thank you, Santa Claus.

For fifty-seven years, the councilman's wife brought honey cakes to the children on Christmas morning, and no one but her husband and Hehheh ever knew where they came from. Only when she was ready to leave this earth, at the ripe age of eighty-four, did she tell her story to the priest. He shared the story with a few children-loving people, and to this day the children of Nebelregen find honey cakes on their doorsteps on Christmas morning.

The End

Hehheh and the Magic Needle
A Story About the Value of Self-Esteem

One day Hehheh realized that his only coat needed mending. He went to a village tailor and said, "I'll bring you a load of kindling wood if you mend my coat."

"You don't need to bring me kindling wood," said the tailor. "Sit down and keep me company, and I'll mend your coat for nothing."

Hehheh sat down, and they joked and laughed together while the tailor mended the coat. But after a while the tailor began to sigh and said, "Oh, Hehheh, here we are joking and laughing, but actually I have little to laugh about. Do you think anyone in this forsaken village ever asks me to make a new suit, or a jacket, or a coat? No, the tailor in the next village gets all the well-paying jobs, while I end up with the mending."

Hehheh looked at the tailor's stitches. They were slovenly and uneven. No wonder no one wanted to entrust good cloth to his careless hands, even though he was a likable fellow. Hehheh began to wonder how he could help him.

When the coat was mended he thanked the tailor and left, but three days later he came back and said, "I found a magic needle for you. If you keep it shiny and sew only the finest of stitches, it will bring you wealth and prosperity."

"A magic needle," laughed the tailor. "Hehheh, where would you find a magic needle?"

"You don't have to take it," replied Hehheh. "But if I were you I would at least see what it can do."

Not wishing to hurt Hehheh's feelings, the tailor took the needle and threaded it. He was just about to mend the lining of an old jacket when he saw a woman and a little girl walking past his window.

The little girl, who wore a lovely blue skirt and a wide-sleeved embroidered blouse, walked at her mother's hand to make sure nothing would happen to her fine outfit. Suddenly a runaway horse came galloping down the narrow street.

Terrified that they might get hurt, the mother and the child jumped across the drainage ditch and pressed themselves against the fence. Luckily a brave man rushed into the horse's path and stopped it from running any farther.

As soon as the danger was over the woman jumped back on the street, holding out her hand to the little girl. Neither of them noticed that one of the girl's wide sleeves had gotten caught on a protruding fence nail. As she

reached for her mother's hand the nail ripped the delicate material from the wristband to the shoulder.

The child began to wail, and the mother scolded, "You careless thing, didn't you notice that your blouse was caught? Oh, what are we going to do? We can't go to the mayor's wife's birthday party with a ripped sleeve."

"Tailor, there is a job for you," said Hehheh.

"I don't think I can sew a seam fine enough to mend a rip like that," replied the tailor sadly. "I got used to sewing only rough stuff."

"A lazy man is full of excuses," replied Hehheh. "'I can't go to work,' he says. 'If I go outside I might meet a lion in the street and get killed.'"

"I have heard those words before," sighed the tailor. "I guess you are right. I must go and offer my services."

He ran outside to the still scolding woman and said, "Ma'am, I'll be glad to mend your little girl's sleeve."

"Don't they call you Tailor Longstitch?" said the woman angrily. "I wouldn't let you mend a horse's blanket, much less a fine sleeve like that. Everybody knows what slovenly work you do."

The tailor's eyes grew misty, and he stammered, "B-b-but I have a magic needle. Let me show you what it can do." He quickly got hold of the girl's wide sleeve and began to sew up the tear with the finest stitches ever seen.

Watching him with amazement, the woman said, "Tailor, either people have been telling me lies about you, or you really have a magic needle. If you finish the job as well as you began it, I will pay you good money."

"I'll try my best," stammered the tailor, and he continued to mend the sleeve with almost invisible stitches. When he was done the woman handed him a ducat and said, "My dear tailor, this is all I am carrying with me right now. I'll send you another ducat tomorrow."

The tailor, who hadn't seen a whole ducat in months, laughed happily and replied, "Ah, but one ducat is more than enough for just one seam."

"Don't be a fool," chided the woman. "I know that this seam is worth two ducats. Ask people to pay you for what you are worth or else they will cheat you, and call you a fool to boot. Now I thank you for coming to my aid, and I will tell all my friends what fine work you do."

With the little girl dancing happily beside her, the woman walked off to the mayor's wife's party. Jumping with joy, the tailor ran back into his room and shouted, "Hehheh, look, I got a whole ducat, and tomorrow I'll get another one. It's all because you gave me a magic needle. Let's go to the inn, and I'll treat you to a glass of wine."

But Hehheh shook his head and got up, and as he walked out the door he said quietly, "Don't let the sparkle and the smooth taste of strong wine deceive you. For in the end it bites like a poisonous snake, and remember, keep the needle shiny, or it will lose its magic."

As the tailor watched Hehheh walking down the street he knocked himself on his forehead and muttered, "Hehheh's right, I really shouldn't go to the inn and waste my money. I should start sewing and keep the needle shiny." But what was he to sew? The lining of the jacket was still to be mended but that took him only a few minutes. What else could he do?

He looked around and suddenly his eyes fell on a sack filled with remnants and old clothes that he used for patching. Hehheh could use a new coat, thought the tailor. His is so old and threadbare it can barely keep him warm. I'll make him one from my remnants.

No sooner had he thought this than he began to cut squares from the remnants and stitch them carefully together. By evening he had enough material to cut out the coat and the lining. The following day he went into the fields and gathered tufts of wool that the sheep had rubbed off on the bushes and trees by the wayside. He took them home and washed them, and used them for padding. By the time the coat was done it was good enough for a king.

A few days later Hehheh came back to town. He stopped at the tailor's to bring him some rare and delicious mushrooms.

After the tailor had fried them and they had eaten, he brought out the coat and said proudly, "Hehheh, look what I have for you." Hehheh was so pleased he didn't know what to say. After hugging the tailor, he put on the coat and walked down the village street.

He had barely gone half a mile when two women came running after him shouting, "Hehheh, where did you get that beautiful coat?"

"Your village tailor made it for me," replied Hehheh proudly. "I'm sure he will make one for you if you ask him."

"Tailor Longstitch made that coat for you?" cried the women.

"Take my word for it," chuckled Hehheh. "I wouldn't lie to you."

"No, you wouldn't," laughed the women, and they ran to the tailor and begged him to make them the same kind of coat. Soon the tailor was overrun with orders for padded patchwork coats, and in time he saved up enough money to buy a house and get married.

A year later his wife asked him to make a padded patchwork blanket for their baby, and it turned out so beautifully that all the women who saw it wanted to have padded patchwork blankets for their babies.

Because the tailor couldn't make them all, he set up a school and taught the women to make their own. Since then thousands of children have slept under padded patchwork blankets. Folks call them quilts now, and as they make them they sing,

> Stick the needle in and out.
> That's what quilting's all about.
> Get to work and do not linger.
> Watch that you don't prick your finger.

The End

❖

Hehheh and the Fisherman

A Story About the Values of Responsibility and Trustworthiness

One day Hehheh went to see his friend the fisherman. The fisherman greeted him happily and said, "I am just about to check out my nets. Would you come along and help me to bail the water out of my boat?"

"I'll come along if you treat me to a fine fish," replied Hehheh.

"You know I always give you a fish when you come to see me," grinned the fisherman. "Hop in and let's go."

They jumped into the boat and took off. As they were drifting downstream they had to bail out quite a lot of water, and after a while Hehheh said, "You could use a new boat. This one looks like it won't last much longer."

The fisherman frowned and replied sadly, "My neighbor has a fine boat he wants to sell. I gave him a down payment, but it will be a while before I can pay off the boat and take possession of it. Whenever I have a bit of money saved something unforeseen happens, and I have to spend it."

Soon they came to the first net. The fisherman pulled it up, but all he found was an old boot. Hehheh threw it back into the river and said, "That fish is too tough to eat."

"Don't fuss," said the fisherman. "We'll find plenty of fish in the other nets."

They rowed on, and checked the second net. This time they found a piece of driftwood. Hehheh laid it on the bottom of the boat and said, "That one would break my teeth."

"Stop joking," griped the fisherman. "I promise we will find some fish." The next net held a dead cat.

"That's not my kind of catfish," said Hehheh.

The fisherman spat three times into the river and replied firmly, "Hehheh, I said we will find some fish. I always find some fish."

Hehheh just grinned, and when they came to the next net and found a rat, Hehheh looked at it and asked, "Is that a ratfish?"

"Cut it out," cried the fisherman. "Stick to your bailing and let's row to the last net. All I can say is, if Lady Luck doesn't smile on us, Lord Wind-in-the-purse and Lady Long-face will dance in my house tonight."

He rowed on, and when they came to the last net he found that Lady Luck was with him after all. The net was full of the finest fish they had ever seen. The fisherman handed Hehheh the first fish out of the net and cried happily, "Hehheh, have you ever seen anything like it? Here, take this fish, it's yours." But Hehheh handed the fish back and replied, "Put it in the tub till later. I'd like to come along and help you sell the rest."

They rowed back to shore, put the tub on a cart, and pulled it to the market. Soon the cook of the wealthiest merchant in town came up to their cart. He looked at the fish and said arrogantly, "Put those fish into my bucket. My master is giving a banquet tonight, and I will need all of them."

The fisherman put all but one fish into the cook's bucket and handed it to him. The cook took it, but when he saw that one fish was still in the tub he sniffed and repeated, "Didn't you hear what I said? I said I want all of them."

"Those are all I have," replied the fisherman.

"How can you say that?" shouted the cook angrily. "Can't you see there is one more fish in the tub?"

"The fish in the tub is Hehheh's fish," explained the fisherman. "I cannot give it to you. I already gave it to him." But the cook was used to getting his way and he shouted, "Who cares about Hehheh. I said I want all the fish."

Most fishermen would have given in, but this fisherman was a pretty independent fellow. He looked at the cook and replied, "You can't have it. I promised it to my friend Hehheh, and a promise is a promise."

His words did not impress the cook at all. He stomped his foot and shouted, "Then keep the other ones, too, you stupid moron. Who needs them? I certainly don't. You are not the only fisherman in this market." He dumped the fish from his bucket back into the fisherman's tub and walked away.

The fisherman wiped his brow. More people came by and looked at the fish, but none of them bought any. After a while the fisherman began to pace back and forth in front of the cart, muttering, "I wonder what's going on. I thought these fish would sell like hotcakes."

While his back was turned, Hehheh took a fish out of the tub and put it in one of the big side pockets of his coat. A few moments later the cook of the duke's general came by. He looked at the fish and said haughtily, "These look halfway decent. I want all of them."

When the fisherman dumped all the fish but one into his bucket, the same thing happened. The cook frowned and said, "Didn't I say I want all of them?" Once again the fisherman explained patiently that he didn't own all of them any longer.

He could have saved his breath because now the cook wanted the fish in the tub more than before. He became very excited and shouted, "Fisherman, I want all of them, and I will pay you double the price."

Although the fisherman needed the money badly he wasn't going to give in. He glared at the cook and repeated through clenched teeth, "I meant what I said when I said one of them belongs to Hehheh."

How could a mere fisherman say no to the duke's general's cook? The cook was disgusted. Waving his arms like windmills he snarled, "I'll give you three times the price of the fish if you give me all of them, and that is my last offer."

Before the fisherman could reply, Hehheh jumped up. He grabbed the last fish, threw it into the cook's bucket, and said, "Sold." But the fisherman wouldn't have it. He stared at Hehheh and screamed, "No, no, Hehheh. Don't you understand that a promise is a promise?" But Hehheh just grinned and turned a bit, so the fisherman could see that something was moving in Hehheh's pocket. A surprised smile appeared on his face and he said to the cook, "If Hehheh says you can have the fish it's all right with me." Smiling triumphantly, the duke's general's cook counted out the money, and left with all the fish.

When he was gone the fisherman slapped Hehheh on his back and shouted, "Hehheh, you have more brains in your little finger than I have in my big old head. Look! I made more money today than I ever made before. In fact, it is just the amount of money I still need to buy the new boat. Come home with me and let's celebrate."

Hehheh was more than willing. He put his fish back into the big tub, and they went to the fisherman's house. After they had told their story, the fisherman's wife fried Hehheh's fish, and they ate and ate and all of them had more than enough. That afternoon the fisherman bought the boat from his neighbor and he and Hehheh and the family took a joyride down the river.

The End

Hehheh and the Hay
A Story About the Values of Responsibility and Kindness

One day Hehheh passed a big meadow where a farm family was trying to rescue their nice dry hay from an approaching thunderstorm. It seemed to be an impossible task. As they frantically raked the hay into heaps and loaded it on the wagon, the clouds were getting darker by the minute, and lightning flashed across the sky.

Without being asked, Hehheh grabbed a pitchfork, and within a short time the wagon was filled to the top with hay. The family had never seen anyone work so fast. While the farmer and his son rushed back to the farm to unload the wagon, Hehheh helped the wife and the daughter to rake up the rest of the hay.

When the men returned, the new heaps were ready to be loaded. With Hehheh helping, the task was soon completed, and everybody climbed on top of the wagon and raced home. Once again Hehheh pitched in. While the wife and the daughter were busy unharnessing the horses, he single-handedly forked the hay from the wagon to the loft. All the farmer and his son had to do was to stash it away.

As they were coming to the end of their task the farmer said, "I didn't think we would get it in before the rain. But we made it."

"I can hardly wait to see our neighbors' faces," snickered his son. "They will be as mad as hornets when they hear that we got our hay in and their's is still out there getting wet." The farmer and his wife chuckled, but Hehheh didn't. He put down his pitchfork, jumped off the wagon and walked toward the cowshed.

As he passed the daughter he said, "I am glad you didn't laugh about your brother's unkind words. A good person is not only concerned about the welfare of his neighbors but also about the welfare of his neighbors' animals."

When no more hay was forthcoming the farmer looked down from the loft and said, "It looks like Hehheh is taking a break. I'll go down to the wagon and take over." But before he could fork up the rest of the hay a sudden whirlwind swept across the farmyard. It lifted the hay from the wagon and scattered it all over the place.

Of course, no one could let good hay go to waste, especially since it hadn't started to rain yet. Father, mother, son, and daughter all began to run hither and yon trying to grab the flying hay. But as they picked it off the ground, big clumps of hay came flying out of the loft. No one had ever seen anything like it.

Suddenly a loud thunderclap shook the Earth, and a flash of lightning as bright as the sun illuminated the sky. "Go inside, everyone go inside," shouted the farmer. Everyone ran into the house. As they huddled around the kitchen table the farmer noticed that Hehheh was missing. "Where is Hehheh?" he scolded. "Is he trying to get himself killed?"

"I saw him going to the cowshed," replied the daughter. "He's probably talking to Moolicka. She gets nervous during thunderstorms."

Soon the rain came down in torrents, and the farmer moaned, "Our hay will be wasted. I wish we had left it out in the meadow."

"Can anyone tell me how our hay could fly out of the loft again?" asked the farm wife. Nobody could answer her question.

When the rain finally stopped the farmer said, "Let's go and see if there is some hay left. We can dry it on the threshing floor. It won't taste good, but it will be better than nothing." They walked outside and couldn't believe their eyes. There was not a single handful of hay in the farmyard. It was a terrible blow.

"The storm must have blown the hay all over the village," said the son.

"I don't think so," replied his sister. "I think it is up in the loft."

"Did you take a deep breath and blow it back into the loft?" sneered the brother. "I'll give you a dollar if you show me how you did it."

"Keep your measly dollar," laughed the daughter. "I'll go and check." She climbed up the ladder to the loft and soon after the family heard her shouting, "Come up here, the hay is all up here." They rushed to the loft and indeed the hay was there. All neatly stacked and still warm from the summer sun.

"I saw the hay flying out of the loft," cried the farm wife. "Remember, I asked how that could happen."

"I think I know what happened," replied the daughter. "Remember when you all laughed because our neighbors didn't get their hay in on time? Hehheh didn't like that. I saw him put down his pitchfork, and as he walked to the cowshed he said, 'A good person is not only concerned about the welfare of his neighbors, he is also concerned about the welfare of his neighbors' animals.' I think Hehheh made us run for our hay because we laughed about the misfortune of our neighbors."

"That is hard to believe," cried the brother. "How could Hehheh have done that?"

"Your sister is right," replied the farmer. "I saw what I saw, and how he did it I will never know. But I know now that I acted like a fool, and Hehheh taught me a lesson. Tomorrow I will go and help our neighbors turn their hay and bring it in when it is dry."

"We'll all help," cried his wife. "And if Hehheh ever comes around again I'll cook him a nice dinner and thank him for saving our hay. He could just as well have let it go to waste."

"He probably saved it more for Moolicka's sake than for us," laughed the daughter, and I think she was right.

The End

Hehheh and the Mayor

A Story About the Value of Respect

One day Hehheh passed a village church. A new bell had just arrived, and the men were getting ready to pull it up to the belfry. It was a big event. Everyone from the village was there to watch, and the women were setting up tables so they could serve a celebration dinner when the task was done.

Hehheh, who liked to go to church, walked up to the mayor and asked, "Could you use a pair of extra hands?"

The mayor, a conceited, grouchy old man, had little patience for ordinary people, and less for the ones, like Hehheh, who were different. He scowled at Hehheh and snapped, "Beat it, Hehheh, don't bother me. This is work for real men."

"Pride usually ends in destruction, while humility ends in honor," muttered Hehheh, and he walked on down the road. Soon after, the men began to hoist the bell up to the belfry.

"Heave, ho, heave, ho," chanted the mayor, and all went well until the bell was halfway up the church tower. Suddenly, for no reason whatsoever, the bell would not go any farther.

The men pulled and pulled. Some ran for extra ladders. Some ran for extra ropes, and all of them including the mayor, said a lot of unholy words that day. After a lot of useless efforts and much idle chattering a child spoke up and said, "Mr. Mayor, you shouldn't have sent Hehheh away. He could have helped us."

"Don't you tell me what I should do, you ill-mannered little lout," scolded the mayor. "What could that worthless little tramp do that we can't do?"

All the people around him gasped, and one of the village elders said, "Mr. Mayor, let me get him. There is more to Hehheh than the eye can see."

"I didn't think you believed in those foolish tales about Hehheh," shouted the mayor. "Go and get him then. You'll soon find out that he can't do anything we can't do."

The village elder didn't bother to contradict the mayor. He ran after Hehheh as fast as he could. Before long he saw Hehheh walking leisurely down the road.

"Hehheh, the bell is stuck. Please come and help us," pleaded the village elder. Hehheh kept on walking. The village elder ran faster, trying to catch up with him, but no matter how hard he ran, he always stayed a couple hundred feet behind. At last he returned to the church and told the mayor what had happened.

"Forget about Hehheh," barked the mayor. "Didn't I tell you that he was a worthless tramp? We'll find a way to get that blasted bell up to the belfry."

"Oh no we won't," cried the men, who were holding on to the ropes. "You go and get Hehheh."

"Who is the boss around here?" yelled the enraged mayor.

"We are!" cried the men in one accord. "Now go and get Hehheh, or we will find us another mayor."

What could the mayor do but rush after Hehheh. Soon he too saw him leisurely walking down the road. Too proud to ask for help, the mayor called out to him, "Hehheh, I want you to come to our celebration dinner."

Hehheh didn't seem to hear him. The mayor began to run faster and faster. Sweat was pouring down his brow, and he was gasping for breath, but although Hehheh seemed constantly within calling distance, he could not catch up with him.

Finally the mayor understood what everybody else had known for a long time. Hehheh was not a worthless little tramp. Hehheh was someone. What Hehheh was the mayor never figured out, but he knew when he needed help.

Making his voice sound as sweet as honey, he called, "Hehheh, I'm sorry I was rude to you."

This time Hehheh heard him, and he sat down by the wayside. But the mayor still had to do some running, and by the time he reached Hehheh his pride had melted away like butter on a hot summer day.

Totally out of breath he panted, "Please Hehheh, we need you."

"It's work for real men," chuckled Hehheh. "Why would you need me?"

"Hehheh," pleaded the mayor, getting down on his knees. "Please, I'll lose my job unless you help us to get the bell to the belfry."

The sight of the proud mayor on his knees begging made Hehheh smile. He got up and returned with the mayor. But Hehheh never helped to pull the bell up to the belfry. Just as they entered the churchyard the men, who had been holding on to the ropes all this time, felt a slight tremor.

They pulled and lo, they were able to pull the bell up to the belfry in the shortest of time. Their cheers could be heard miles away. Everybody danced around, and people kept slapping each other's shoulders until their bones were sore.

How it happened that the bell got struck, and if it had anything to do with Hehheh, no one will ever know. But after the task was done, everyone sat down and ate, and the mayor insisted that Hehheh sit next to him.

They got to know one another that evening, and when it was time to leave Hehheh and the mayor parted as friends.

The End

Part II
Stories to Act Out

When children become storytellers they change from passive listeners to active participants. They learn to give their own interpretation of the story characters and gain the courage to step in front of their classmates. As their classmates respond to a funny or dramatic rendition, their own confidence grows in leaps and bounds, and a new storyteller is born.

The stories in this part are carefully chosen to teach children to become storytellers. Here is an example of what I do with the story of "The Farmer and the Stork" (see page 93).

1. Storyteller Ruthilde picks three students to play the parts of the stork, the crane, and the farmer and seats them in chairs facing the audience.

2. Storyteller Ruthilde begins to narrate the story. Each time the stork is to say something, Ruthilde goes to the stork, tells him what to say, and asks him to repeat or paraphrase her words. She uses the same method with the farmer and the crane.

3. Before Ruthilde and the students retell the story, Ruthilde conducts a class discussion on how to enhance the story with movement, facial expressions, and different voices. A stork speaks with a hoarse voice and walks in majestic fashion. A crane walks with shorter steps and has a buglelike voice. The farmer shakes his fist, frowns, and speaks with an angry voice.

4. After a brief review of lines, movements, and voices, Ruthilde and the three students retell the story.

5. After the retelling of the story, the listeners are invited to tell what they liked about the rendition. Then they decide if they want another group to retell the story or to put the story into a different setting. For example, the stork becomes a boy called Roni, the crane becomes a boy called Jovi, and the farmer becomes Police Officer Passauf. The students pick a crime. Roni and Jovi either steal a car, use drugs, or shoplift. Here is a synopsis of a different version of the story. This time the students create their own dialogues.

Storyteller:
> Roni strolls down the street. He is bored. He meets Jovi, who is also bored.

Dialogue 1:
> Jovi suggests breaking into a car. Roni hesitates, but Jovi convinces him to do it.

Storyteller:
> As they career through a 30-mile per hour zone at 75 miles per hour, they get caught by Officer Passauf.

Dialogue 2:
> Officer Passauf arrests them. Roni tries to explain that it was Jovi's idea and that he was only a bystander, but Officer Passauf reacts like the farmer and takes them both to court.

This could be the end of the story, but most of the time the students decide to go on with the story and they add Roni and Jovi's parents, two witnesses, a judge, a jury, and a foreman (the jury usually turns out to be the whole class).

Dialogue 3:
    Roni calls his parents. Jovi calls his parents.

(Because Roni and Jovi's parents are not present, it is a one-sided conversation. Roni and Jovi have to imagine their parents' response and form answers that will convey their parents' reactions to their classmates.)

Storyteller:
    The parents jump into a car and drive to the police station.

Dialogue 4:
    Roni and his parents talk. Jovi and his parents talk. Officer Passauf tells what he has to do.

Storyteller:
    Roni, Jovi, Officer Passauf, and the parents go to court, where a judge, a lawyer, two witnesses, and a jury foreman are waiting for them.

Because most of the students have watched countless court scenes on television, I turn the court scene over to them and only guide and time it with my narrations. The verdict is the same as in the story of "The Farmer and the Stork." Roni was caught with Jovi and ends up in jail with Jovi.

We usually finish the session by writing advisory letters to Roni and Jovi. But before we start writing we talk about Roni and Jovi's problems. How did Roni and Jovi get into trouble? In general, trouble can be caused by what? (Write students' suggestions on the chalkboard.) Thoughtlessness, ignorance, hatred, greediness, poverty, indifference, addiction, prejudice, sickness, natural disasters, war, death. Trouble is often caused by circumstances beyond our control. No one is immune to trouble. (Here is an opportunity for the storyteller to share a personal problem story and how he or she solved it.)

What can Roni and Jovi do to solve their problems and get out of trouble? What can we do to help people like Roni and Jovi? Do other countries (or generations) have the same problems we have? One can discuss a multitude of questions in connection with the story of "The Farmer and the Stork."

After the students have written their letters, the storyteller takes them home and writes a brief response to each one. At the next session (if the students agree to it) the storyteller reads the letters to the class.

Helping the students to express their feelings, look for resolution, and develop their storytelling skills is an exciting method of teaching because one rarely meets a student who is not interested in acting out stories. Most of them clamor for the leading roles.

The Three Languages
A Story About the Values of Courage and Caring

Characters: *Storyteller, Patron, Nephew, Home-Mother, Anuke, Teacher, Cat, Frog, Father, Boy, Old Woman, Ghost Dog, Crow, King, and Dove.*

Storyteller:
> In a small village lived long ago a wealthy patron who liked to spend his money on good causes. One day he came to the small cottage where the villagers housed the orphans and said to the home-mother,

Patron:
> I have no one to leave my money to but a nephew who can hardly wait until I die. Do you have a smart boy who would benefit from an education? I have heard of a celebrated teacher in the city who can teach more than is normally taught in schools, and I would like to send him a pupil.

Storyteller:
> The home-mother was delighted, and she replied,

Home-Mother:
> We have a number of very smart children who would profit from an education. But the smartest of them is a girl by the name of Anuke. She learns so quickly that our local schoolmaster insists that he cannot teach her another thing.

Storyteller:
> The patron looked amazed and said,

Patron:
> I didn't know girls could be smarter than boys. By all means send her. I shall give you the address of the teacher and the money to pay him. I trust that you will do everything to my satisfaction. My only request is that the girl comes to me at the end of the school year and tells me what she has learned.

Storyteller:
> When the patron was gone the home-mother called Anuke and said,

Home-Mother:
> Anuke, my prayers for you have been answered. You are going to study with a celebrated teacher in the city.

79

Storyteller:

Eager to learn, Anuke went to the city, and, after an initial examination, the teacher said,

Teacher:

Anuke, you are smarter than any girl I have ever met. How would you like to learn the language of the frogs?

Storyteller:

Anuke's face lit up and she said happily,

Anuke:

I have always wanted to learn the language of the frogs.

Storyteller:

So she got busy and studied day in and day out. When the year was up Anuke went to the patron's house and was introduced to him and his nephew. The patron asked her kindly,

Patron:

Anuke, I have heard that you are a very smart girl. Tell me what you have learned this year?

Storyteller:

Anuke smiled happily and replied,

Anuke:

Oh kind and generous sir, my teacher taught me the language of the frogs.

Storyteller:

The patron began to laugh. Slapping his knees he shouted,

Patron:

Splendid! Splendid! My money could not have been spent on anything more useful.

Storyteller:

But the nephew's face turned purple and he hissed,

Nephew:

Uncle, I cannot believe what I am hearing. How can you waste your precious money on such utter foolishness? The language of frogs! Who ever heard of something so utterly useless. I suggest that you sue that man and send this girl back to the orphans' cottage.

Storyteller:

Amused at his nephew's rage, the patron smiled and replied,

Patron:

And I suggest that you save your breath, dear nephew. Once I am under the ground you can do with my money what you want to do. Right now I spend it as I wish. I will send Anuke to this man for a second year.

Storyteller:

Anuke thanked her patron and went back to her beloved teacher. When she returned the following year, the patron asked,

Patron:

And what did you learn this year, dear Anuke?

Storyteller:

Anuke replied excitedly,

Anuke:

Oh kind sir, this time my teacher taught me the languages of the dogs and cats.

Storyteller:

Before the patron could comment his nephew shrieked,

Nephew:

Did I hear you right? Did you say you studied the languages of dogs and cats? Tell me, do mutts talk differently than mongrels? Uncle, this is insane. The teacher is deranged. He is out of his mind. Spending your precious money on an imbecile like him is the craziest thing I have ever seen.

Storyteller:

But the patron laughed and replied,

Patron:

Nephew, calm yourself. If you carry on like that you will die before I do. There will be enough money for you to waste, but while I still have my faculties I intend to enjoy myself. Who knows? I might go back to the school bench myself. It is my will and command that Anuke go to school for yet another year, provided she wishes to go.

Storyteller:

The nephew jumped up and ran out the door muttering,

Nephew:

I am going to have to leave or else I will lose my mind.

Storyteller:

But Anuke's face lit up like the sun, and she cried,

Anuke:

Oh dearest sir, how can I ever thank you. My teacher promised to teach me the languages of the birds. Do come along and study them with me. They promise to be the most interesting, most versatile languages of all.

Storyteller:

But the patron shook his head and said sorrowfully,

Patron:

I deeply regret that I cannot go with you. Because I have no children of my own, I promised my sister on her deathbed that her son would be my heir. Little did I know what a covetous and greedy man he would become. If I don't watch out he will find a way to rob me blind, and I would truly hate to die in the poorhouse.

Storyteller:

Touched by his sorrow, Anuke said,

Anuke:

If I can help it you will not die in a poorhouse.

Storyteller:

Anuke spent a challenging year at her teacher's house. The languages of all the birds were extremely difficult to learn. But when the year was up he sent her away with the highest marks he had ever given to a student. Eager to report to her patron, she returned to the village. But when she came to the orphans' cottage, the home-mother said,

Home-Mother:

Oh Anuke, a month ago your dear patron became very ill. While he was laying in bed with a high fever his wicked nephew stole all his money and disappeared. A neighbor heard him moaning and saw to it that he was taken to the city hospital for the poor.

Storyteller:

Deeply upset, Anuke decided to go back to the city to find a way to help her beloved patron. But when the home-mother offered to pay the coach fare her cat said in cat language,

Cat:

Purr, purrroo, it would be a pity,
If Anuke took a coach to the great big city.
As she travels along the dusty street,
She'll do well if she walks on her own two feet.

Storyteller:
Anuke stroked the cat's back and went on her way. Toward evening she passed a lake. Tired from all the walking she sat down and put her feet into the cool water. Suddenly she saw a little frog with an injured leg. She bent down and said,

Anuke:
Poor little thing, isn't there a way to help you?

Storyteller:
The frog replied in frog language,

Frog:
Go to the other side of the lake and look for a plant with red and yellow blossoms. Bring a few blossoms back to me and lay them on my injured leg.

Storyteller:
Anuke did as the frog had told her, and when she put the blossoms on the frog's leg, it healed immediately. The frog thanked her and said,

Frog:
You helped me and now I will help you. Down the road in a big house with a blue tile roof lives a sick little boy. If you make some tea from the same blossoms and give it to the boy, he will become well.

Storyteller:
Anuke thanked the frog, picked some of the blossoms, and ventured on down the road. Soon after she came to the house. She knocked at the door and said,

Anuke:
I was told that there is a sick little boy living here. I might be able to help.

Storyteller:
But the boy's father replied sadly,

Father:
So many have tried, but all of their efforts were useless.

Storyteller:
Just then Anuke heard the boy cry,

Boy:
Who is there? I want to see who is there.

Storyteller:

The father shrugged his shoulders and led Anuke into the boy's bedroom.

Storyteller:

The boy took an instant liking to Anuke and said,

Boy:

Stay awhile and tell me your story.

Storyteller:

Anuke sat down and began to tell him how she had learned the languages of frogs, dogs, cats, and birds and how she had healed the little frog's injury. The minute the boy heard about the frog he cried,

Boy:

I dreamt about a frog last night. Please make me well, too.

Storyteller:

With the permission of the boy's parents Anuke went into the kitchen and brewed the tea. As soon as the boy had swallowed a cupful of tea he began to feel better. He kept drinking one cupful after another, and the next morning he sat up in his bed for the first time in weeks.

The parents were delighted and filled up a sack with money and gave it to Anuke. But Anuke begged them to send it to the city hospital for the poor with the instructions to use the money for her patron's care.

Glad that she had been able to help her patron, Anuke went on her way. Toward evening she came to a house in the forest. She knocked at the door, and an old woman answered and asked,

Old Woman:

For goodness sake, what are you doing alone in the forest?

Storyteller:

Anuke replied,

Anuke:

Please, kind old woman, I am an honest traveler. Could I spend the night at your house?

Storyteller:

The old woman replied sadly,

Old Woman:

You may, but you will not get much sleep. Every evening when the sun goes down a ghost dog appears and howls all through the night. It sounds so terrible it has driven the owners out of this house. I am only staying here because I have nowhere else to go.

Storyteller:

Anuke put her arms around the old woman's shoulders and replied,

Anuke:

You won't have to stay alone this night. I think I can help. I know the language of dogs. Maybe I can find out what is bothering the ghost dog.

Storyteller:

Glad that someone was willing to help, the old woman allowed her to stay. That night the ghost dog howled like he had never howled before.

Ghost Dog:

Ow bow wow.

Storyteller:

When morning came Anuke said,

Anuke:

An ancestor of the family who owned this house was a forest robber who murdered unsuspecting travelers and stole their money. As a punishment he has to come back in the shape of a ghost dog and howl every night until someone digs up the money he stole and shares it with others.

Storyteller:

The old woman contacted the owners of the house, and they searched and found the money. They divided it in three parts. One part for the poor, one part for Anuke and the old woman, and one part for themselves. Anuke sent her part as a gift to the home-mother and the orphans.

The following day she continued her journey to the city. Toward noon she came to a big tree and sat in its shadow to eat her lunch. Soon a crow came flying along and looked hungrily at the bread. Anuke broke off a piece and began to feed her. When the bread was gone the crow said,

Crow:

Run to the city and stand in front of the castle. The king is going to abdicate and choose a successor.

Storyteller:

Anuke followed the crow's advice. When she arrived at the city she found hundreds of young men already there. When the clock struck twelve, the castle door swung open, and out came the old king, holding a dove in his hands. Stroking the dove's wings the king said to her,

King:

Dove of mine fly out of my hand,
Find a wise ruler for this land.

Storyteller:

The dove flew over the assembled crowd and landed on Anuke's shoulders, singing,

Dove:

Rooke, deekoo, rooke, deekoo,
Oh, King, I found a successor for you.

Storyteller:

The crowd began to cheer, and Anuke was led to the king, who said,

King:

I am old and I would like to retire. Because my dove has chosen you to be the queen of this land, I know my country will be in good hands.

Storyteller:

Anuke became a very fine queen because she had many helpers. Her kind patron, who had recovered from his illness, became one of her councillors. The cats got rid of all the varmints. The frogs told her of upcoming droughts. The dogs tracked down all the evildoers, including the nephew, and the birds informed her of everything that happened in the world.

But best of all, with a caring young queen in the castle, the people, too, began to care for each other, which enhanced everyone's life greatly.

The End

The Elephant and the Monkey
A Story About the Values of Cooperation and Respect

Characters: *Storyteller, Goat, Gnu, Dog, Monkey, Elephant, and Owl.* (The characters sit in a row facing the children. The children help with the rhymes.)

Storyteller:
> One morning a Fulani man put his goat out to graze. Goat tried to eat, but the grass behind the Fulani man's hut was so hard and dry that Goat jumped over the thorn hedge and walked off to look for better pasture.
>
> After a while Goat came to a stone hill. Only a few herbs grew on it, but they looked good to Goat and she began to eat them. As she ate her way to the top of the hill she did not watch where she was going, and suddenly Goat's foot got caught between two big stones.
>
> Goat knew the vultures would come and eat her if she didn't get her foot out. So Goat began to bleat for help.

Goat:
> Help me, help me, set me free,
> Before the vultures make a meal of me.

Storyteller:
> After a while Gnu came along. When he saw that Goat's foot was caught between two stones he said,

Gnu:
> Poor Goat, let me see if I can't push the stones apart.

Storyteller:
> Gnu pushed and pushed and pushed, but the stones didn't budge one inch. When Goat realized that Gnu wasn't strong enough to push the stones apart, she bleated again,

Goat:
> (*Children join in.*) Help me, help me, set me free,
> Before the vultures make a meal of me.

Storyteller:
> Soon Dog came along and said,

Dog:
> Goat, you should not have run away from home, but I think I can help you.

Storyteller:
Dog put his teeth around Goat's leg and tried to pull her foot loose. But his teeth scraped the skin off Goat's leg, and Goat began to cry because it hurt so much. Dog stopped pulling, and once again Goat bleated,

Goat:
(Children join in.) Help me, help me, set me free,
Before the vultures make a meal of me.

Storyteller:
Soon Monkey came along, and when he saw the situation he said,

Monkey:
Maybe we can all take hold of Goat's tail and pull her out.

Storyteller:
The animals thought that was a good idea. Monkey grabbed Goat's tail, Gnu grabbed Monkey's tail, Dog grabbed Gnu's tail, and they shouted: *(Mime this part.)*

Monkey, Gnu, and Dog:
One, two, three, pull, pull, pull.

Storyteller:
They pulled and pulled and pulled, and they would still be pulling, but all of a sudden Goat's tail broke in two. Gnu, Dog, and Monkey fell to the ground, with Monkey holding the end piece of Goat's tail in his paws. Poor Goat began to wail,

Goat:
My tail, my tail, my wonderful tail.

Storyteller:
Just then Elephant came along, and he asked,

Elephant:
What is going on?

Storyteller:
Poor Goat sobbed,

Goat:
My foot is stuck between two stones, and no one can help me. Gnu tried to push the stones apart, but he wasn't strong enough. Dog tried to pull my foot loose, but all he did was injure my leg. Monkey suggested that they pull me out by my tail, but all they managed to do was to pull part of my tail off. Oh, what am I going to do?

Storyteller:
Elephant laughed and said,

Elephant:
You all did more harm than good. Let's see what I can do.

Storyteller:

He put his trunk around the biggest stone and lifted it off Goat's foot. The animals cheered and from then on, whenever they met Elephant they greeted him and said,

Dog, Gnu, Goat, and Monkey:

May you live happily, may you live long.
God gave wisdom, God made you strong.

Storyteller:

Unfortunately the animal's praise went to Elephant's head, and one day Elephant began to sing,

Elephant:

Tonkapong, tonkapong, tonkapong.
God made me wise, God made me strong.
Stronger than Monkey, Dog, and Gnu,
There is nothing in the world that I can't do.

Storyteller:

Wherever he went he sang that song. At the watering hole,

Elephant:

(*Children join in.*) Tonkapong, tonkapong, tonkapong,
God made me wise, God made me strong.
Stronger than Monkey, Dog, and Gnu,
There is nothing in the world that I can't do.

Storyteller:

At the clearing,

Elephant:

(*Children join in.*) Tonkapong, tonkapong, tonkapong.
God made me wise, God made me strong.
Stronger than Monkey, Dog, and Gnu,
There is nothing in the world that I can't do.

Storyteller:

In the morning, tonkapong, tonkapong, tonkapong. Late at night, tonkapong, tonkapong, tonkapong. After a while it got on the animals' nerves, and one day Monkey called out to Elephant,

Monkey:

Stop singing that foolish song, Elephant. You know there are things that you can't do.

Storyteller:

Monkey hadn't planned to belittle Elephant. He just didn't want him to be so conceited. So it came as a great surprise to Monkey when Elephant became very angry and said,

Elephant:

You call my song foolish. Let's see who is foolish. Weren't you the one who suggested pulling Goat out by her tail? Ever since you did that Goat has been running around with half of her tail missing. So don't you dare criticize my song.

Storyteller:

Monkey scratched himself behind his ears and said,

Monkey:

Elephant, you know I'm happy you saved Goat's life, but that doesn't mean that you can do everything.

Storyteller:

Elephant glared at Monkey and replied,

Elephant:

Oh yes I can.

Storyteller:

Monkey stared at Elephant and said.

Monkey:

Oh no you can't.

Storyteller:

They shouted yes I can and no you can't till they were hoarse, and finally Monkey said,

Monkey:

Let's go to Owl and see what she says.

Storyteller:

Elephant agreed, and he and Monkey went to Owl. When they got there Monkey said,

Monkey:

Dear Owl, Elephant saved Goat and now he claims that there is nothing in the world he can't do, and I say that's not true. Please be so kind and tell us who is right.

Storyteller:

Owl blinked her eyes and said sleepily,

Owl:

Whooo, whooo, I'll tell you what to do. Not too far from here stands a shea-nut tree with only one fruit on it. You two go and find it; the one who brings me the fruit is right.

Storyteller:

Owl went back to sleep, and Elephant and Monkey went in search of the shea-nut tree. Monkey was the first to spot it, but as he and

Elephant grew nearer, Monkey saw with dismay that the tree stood on the other side of a deep river.

There was no way that Monkey could cross that river, so he sat down and stared into the water. Meanwhile Elephant splashed through the river singing happily,

Elephant:

(Children join in.) Tonkapong, tonkapong, tonkapong.
I've very smart, I'm very strong.
I'm smarter than Monkey, Dog, and Gnu,
I'm doing something that Monkey can't do.

Storyteller:

But when he came to the shea-nut tree he realized that the fruit was on the top branch, way above the ground. Elephant stretched his trunk and tried to reach it. No luck. Elephant put his trunk around the tree trunk and tried to bend it. No luck. Elephant shook the tree. No luck.

Finally Elephant began to think, and he realized how foolish he had been. He ran back to the river, waded to the other side, and said to Monkey,

Elephant:

Monkey, you were foolish when you tried to pull Goat out by her tail, and I was foolish when I insisted that there was nothing in the world I could not do. If I carry you across the river will you climb into the tree and get the fruit for Owl? She is wiser than both of us.

Storyteller:

Monkey patted Elephant's trunk and replied,

Monkey:

Of course I will.

Storyteller:

Elephant carried Monkey across the river, and Monkey climbed to the top of the shea-nut tree and got the fruit for Owl. On their way to Owl's tree they changed Elephant's song, and ever since they have been singing,

Elephant and Owl:

(Children join in.) Tonkapong, tonkapong, tonkapong.
Divided we are weak,
And united we are strong.
Tonkapong, tonkapong, tonkapong.

The End

❖

The Farmer and the Stork

A Story About the Value of Responsibility

Characters: *Storyteller, Stork, Crane, and Farmer.*

Storyteller:
A hungry stork went to the river to find some food. He searched and searched, but luck was not with him. He caught nothing more than a few tiny tadpoles and a lizard. After a while he met a crane, who greeted him and said,

Crane:
A good day to you, friend stork.

Storyteller:
The stork replied crossly,

Stork:
I can't see anything good about the day as long as I am hungry. I haven't found a single frog. Just a few tiny tadpoles and a lizard.

Storyteller:
The crane chuckled and said,

Crane:
There is a field not too far from here with more than enough grain for both of us. Why don't you come with me and eat your fill?

Storyteller:
The stork replied,

Stork:
Does the grain belong to anyone?

Storyteller:
The crane laughed and answered,

Crane:
Who cares. I eat food wherever I find it. Come along, it's time for you to try something different.

Storyteller:

The stork followed the crane, and both of them walked right into a net that the farmer had set to catch the birds that were eating his grain. The farmer wrung the crane's neck but when he reached out for the stork, the stork said,

Stork:

Dear farmer. I beg you to let me live. I am not a crane. I am a stork. I never ate a single grain from your field. I am a very good bird. I just came along with the crane to keep him company.

Storyteller:

The farmer replied,

Farmer:

Did your mother not teach you that it is well to keep out of the way of the wicked, lest you fall into the trap with them? I caught you with the crane and with the crane you must die.

The End

Kannitverstan

A Story About the Value of Humility

Characters: *Storyteller, Tailor Ludwig, Dutchman, Longshoreman, and Mourner.*

Storyteller:
> Many years ago a young German tailor by the name of Ludwig decided to see how tailors in other lands stitched seams and cut cloth. He traveled through many countries and increased his knowledge. On his way home he passed through Amsterdam, a rich and mighty city with one of the busiest harbors in all of Europe.
>
> As Ludwig wandered around admiring the clean streets, one of the fine Dutch houses caught his attention. Its shiny windows were bigger than the door of his father's hut, and the flower boxes in front of those windows had more bright-red and snow-white tulips than Ludwig's mother could raise in her whole garden.
>
> Even the freshly scrubbed marble steps that led up to the big copper door spoke of the great wealth of its owner. Ludwig looked and looked and finally he could not stand it any longer. Turning to a passerby, he asked in his German language,

Ludwig:
> Kannst du mir sagen wem das herrliche Haus gehoert?

Storyteller:
> Which means,

Ludwig:
> Can you tell me who owns that magnificent house?

Storyteller:
> The man, who could not understand Ludwig's question, answered brusquely,

Dutchman:
> Kannitverstan

Storyteller:
> "Kannitverstan" means "I can't understand," but Ludwig, who thought it was the name of the man who owned the house, said to himself,

Ludwig:

Ach, Herr Kannitverstan must be a very rich man. How nice it would be if I had his money and could live in a house like that.

Storyteller:

After a while Ludwig went to the harbor, where he saw hundreds of ships of all sizes waiting to be unloaded. Most of them were big ships, but there was one that dwarfed the rest.

It had just arrived from East India, and the longshoremen were busily unloading its goods. Like an army of ants they rushed in and out, carrying huge boxes and bundles to the wharf. Eager to see how much a ship like that could hold, Ludwig watched for one hour, two hours, three hours, and still they rolled out more and more barrels filled with treasures from all over the world.

Wondering who could be the owner of the ship and all its wealth, Ludwig finally approached one of the longshoremen and asked in his German language,

Ludwig:

Guter Freund, wem gehoert das Schiff und alle seine Gueter?

Storyteller:

Which means,

Ludwig:

Good friend, who owns this ship and all its goods?

Storyteller:

Tired and irritated from all his hard work, the longshoreman snapped,

Longshoreman:

Kannitverstan.

Storyteller:

Ludwig could not believe his ears. He shook his head in wonder and said to himself,

Ludwig:

Kannitverstan, Kannitverstan. Now I know how Herr Kannitverstan could build such a splendid house with all those flower boxes in front of the windows, while a poor devil like me must be content just to have enough money to rent a room.

Storyteller:

Sad and depressed about the unequal distribution of wealth, Ludwig walked slowly away from the harbor. As he turned a corner a funeral procession came his way. Ludwig took off his hat and watched.

Four horses were drawing the funeral wagon, which bore a beautifully decorated coffin. Behind the wagon walked more mourners than Ludwig had ever seen. All of them were dressed in black; some were dry-eyed while others wept loudly, accompanied by the thin wailing sounds of the death bell.

Ludwig stood and stared and wondered who the dead person could be. And then, as all good people do when they see a funeral procession, he began to think of his own demise, and tears gathered in his eyes. Soon they started rolling down his cheeks and, before he could check himself, he tiptoed over to one of the mourners and whispered in German,

Ludwig:

Bitte schoen, wer ist denn die Person die ihr zu Grabe tragt?

Storyteller:

Which means,

Ludwig:

Excuse me, who is the person you are taking to the grave?

Storyteller:

Touched by the tears in Ludwig's eyes, the mourner patted his shoulder and whispered politely,

Mourner:

Kannitverstan.

Storyteller:

Ludwig could not believe his ears. All upset, he cried out,

Ludwig:

Kannitverstan, Kannitverstan. This is the funeral of rich Herr Kannitverstan? I can't believe it. I must go and pay him my last respects.

Storyteller:

He followed the funeral procession and watched sadly as they lowered Herr Kannitverstan into his grave. A few days later he turned his steps toward home. After he arrived and settled down, his favorite story to tell was the story of Herr Kannitverstan, and how all his riches had not saved him from the last road all people must travel.

The End

❖

A Mother's Advice

A Story About the Values of Responsibility and Honesty

Characters: *Storyteller, Prince, Queen, Vizier's Son, General's Son, and Woodcutter.*

Storyteller:
One day a prince came to his mother the queen and said,

Prince:
Mother, I need your help. Being a prince makes it very difficult for me to find a true friend. I never know if people like me for myself or for my station in life.

Storyteller:
The queen replied,

Queen:
My dear son, good and honest friends are a gift from God. But God won't drop them into your lap, you have to look for them. A good way to begin is to ask some of the young men you know to have lunch with you. See to it that three hard-boiled eggs are served to the two of you. After your guest and you have each eaten one egg, offer your guest the third one and observe what he does.

Storyteller:
The prince did as his mother had told him. The first young man he invited was the vizier's son. They spent the morning playing games, and then they sat down for lunch. After each had eaten one egg the prince said,

Prince:
My dear friend, help yourself to the third egg.

Storyteller:
But the vizier's son replied,

Vizier's Son:
Oh no, Your Royal Highness. Even though my egg was the most delicious egg I have ever eaten, I wouldn't think of touching the third egg. You are the prince and you are the one who is entitled to the third egg.

Storyteller:

The next day the prince invited the son of the general. They went hunting and sat down for lunch afterwards. After each had eaten one egg the prince said,

Prince:

I am mighty hungry today, but since you are my guest I want you to have the remaining egg.

Storyteller:

The general's son grabbed the egg and replied,

General's Son:

Those eggs taste mighty good. I could eat ten of them in one sitting.

Storyteller:

The following day the prince disguised himself and put some bread and three hard-boiled eggs into his pocket. He walked through the city and off into the forest. After a while he saw a young woodcutter cutting down a tree. Sweat was pouring from his brow, but he was whistling a happy tune.

The prince asked if he could help him, and soon he was swinging the ax, cutting and stacking wood. When noontime came round the prince said,

Prince:

My friend, I have three eggs and some bread in my pocket. Come and have lunch with me. I would like to talk to you some more.

Storyteller:

The woodcutter accepted his invitation, and they both sat down and ate an egg. When they were done the prince said,

Prince:

There is one more egg left. Would you like to eat it?

Storyteller:

The woodcutter took the egg and peeled it carefully. Then he cut it in half and said,

Woodcutter:

Here, take the other half. I am sure you are just as hungry as I am.

Storyteller:

They shared the egg and talked for a while, and when lunchtime was over they got up and finished the job. When the prince came home to his mother she asked,

Queen:

How did your day go, and did you make any progress in finding a good friend?

Storyteller:

The prince smiled and replied,

Prince:

Mother, I followed your advice, and I learned a few things. The vizier's son said, "I wouldn't think of touching the third egg. You are the prince and you are the one who is entitled to the third egg."

Storyteller:

The queen replied,

Queen:

A king who surrounds himself with men who flatter him lives in the company of dishonest men. What did your second guest do?

Storyteller:

The prince replied,

Prince:

I went hunting with the general's son. When it was time to eat we sat down and ate our eggs. As you told me, I offered him the third egg, and he took it, saying, "Those eggs taste mighty good. I could eat ten of them in one sitting."

Storyteller:

The queen replied,

Queen:

Beware, the root of conflicts between people and countries is often greediness. Many kings have lost their thrones to generals. Tell me about your third guest.

Storyteller:

The prince said,

Prince:

I put on some old clothes and went into the forest. Soon I met a young woodcutter who was working very hard. I asked if I could help him, and we worked well together. At noontime I invited him to share my lunch.

When we each had eaten one egg I offered him the third egg. He took it and peeled it, but he didn't eat it. He cut it in half and said, "Here, take the other half. I am sure you are just as hungry as I am."

Storyteller:

The queen smiled and asked,

Queen:

Tell me, which of the three will you choose for a friend?

Storyteller:

The prince laughed and replied,

Prince:

Mother, a king needs a man he can trust and who will share his ups and downs with him. I hope the woodcutter will become my friend.

Storyteller:

The queen put her arms around the prince and said,

Queen:

A mirror reflects a man's face. But what he is really like is shown by the kind of friends he chooses. Truly a wise son makes his mother happy.

The End

The Nobleman
and the Carrier

A Story About the Values of Respect and Humility

Characters: *Storyteller, Giovanni, Nobleman, Scribe, Judge, and Advocate.*

Storyteller:
>   Since the streets in the city of Venice are too narrow for carts the people used to use carriers to transport everything that needed to be transported. If someone wanted to move from one house to another, carriers were called to carry the household goods.
>
>   If someone bought a big object, he or she called a carrier to carry it home. Carriers were needed at all times, but although those men could tote up to two hundred pounds on their backs their wages were small.
>
>   Some of the carriers were rough and uncouth men, and their customers were afraid to haggle about prices with them. Others who were kind became longtime family friends. One of the kind ones, a man by the name of Giovanni, had a hard time making a living. He could never say no if people came to him and asked for help.
>
>   If someone said, "Giovanni, my dearest friend, may the saints bless you and your family, I am in great trouble. My poor old mother, God bless her soul, is very sick, and I do not have a lire to rent a stretcher. Please for the sake of the holy Mother Mary carry her to the infirmary," Giovanni would do it.
>
>   If he saw an old man or an old woman carrying too heavy a bundle, he would take it from the person's shoulders and carry it. His wife, Anna, scolded him many a time when he came home with barely anything in his pockets, but Giovanni always replied,

Giovanni:
>   He who shuts his ears to the cries of the poor will be ignored in his time of need.

Storyteller:
>   One day his goodness was rewarded in a strange and unusual way. It was a hot summer day, and Giovanni was carrying a huge bundle of goods from one side of the city to the other. As he made his way through the streets he called out,

Giovanni:

Warda! Warda!

Storyteller:

Warda is the Italian word for "watch out," and everybody but an arrogant nobleman moved out of his way. As Giovanni tried to squeeze himself past the conceited fellow, a hook, which had worked its way out of the heavy bundle, got stuck in the nobleman's robe. Nothing happened, but the nobleman flew into a rage and yelled,

Nobleman:

You miserable oaf, you heedless imbecile, I'll see to it that you get a beating with a rope for this. Guards, guards, come and arrest this man.

Storyteller:

Two guards came running, and poor, kind Giovanni was taken to jail. Fortunately the scribe, who took down the complaint of the nobleman, knew Giovanni. He felt pity for him, and the following morning he spoke to the judge.

Scribe:

Your Honor, yesterday a carrier by the name of Giovanni was brought to jail. I know him to be an honest, hard-working man, beloved by the poor and wealthy, and I beg you humbly to assign an advocate to his case.

Storyteller:

The judge, who valued his scribe's opinion, did as he was asked. When the advocate came to Giovanni's prison cell he said to him,

Advocate:

My dear fellow, I would like to help you. But I read the accusations of the nobleman against you, and there is little hope that I can save you from a beating. Tell me exactly what happened.

Storyteller:

Encouraged by the kind words, Giovanni said,

Giovanni:

Honorable advocate, I was carrying a huge bundle of goods through the street, asking everyone to watch out and step out of my way. I do not know why the nobleman did not heed my call. As I tried to squeeze my way past him a hook got caught in his gown, and although it did no harm he had me arrested for carelessness.

I can take a beating, but it will scar my back, and I might never be able to carry another load again.

Storyteller:

The advocate thought for a while, and then he said,

Advocate:

I believe you, but a poor man has few rights in this city. Nevertheless, if you really warned the nobleman I think I can help you. Promise me by the saints and everything that is holy not to open your mouth throughout the trial.

Storyteller:

It was a strange request, but Giovanni trusted the advocate and said,

Giovanni:

I promise.

Storyteller:

The trial took place the next day. The nobleman was the first to state his case, and he said,

Nobleman:

Your Honor, I was walking along the street minding my own business when suddenly this carrier rammed his heavy load of goods into my side. A sharp, pointed hook was sticking out of his slovenly packed load. Had I not had the presence of mind to turn my head the hook would have gouged out my eye.

I was lucky that only my robe got torn, but to set an example I insist that this man be punished for his carelessness and receive a beating.

Storyteller:

The judge, who had a heart for the poor, replied,

Judge:

A beating is a harsh punishment for anyone, but it is harshest for a man who makes his living carrying heavy loads on his back. He would receive so many scars that he would never be able to work again.

Storyteller:

The nobleman stared at the judge and cried out vengefully,

Nobleman:

That is exactly what I want to happen. I could have been blinded by the blundering fool.

Storyteller:

The judge turned to the advocate and said,

Judge:

My dear advocate, please cross-examine the defendant.

Storyteller:
The advocate stepped forward and said to Giovanni,

Advocate:
Giovanni, you are aware of the seriousness of the charge against you. You now have a chance to tell your story.

Storyteller:
When Giovanni remained silent, the advocate turned to the judge and said,

Advocate:
Your Honor, I cannot defend a man who cannot tell me his side of the story. He obviously is unable to speak for himself.

Storyteller:
The nobleman jumped up from his chair and yelled at Giovanni,

Nobleman:
You knave, you rogue. Don't you dare put on a show. You were perfectly able to talk yesterday. I heard you yell "Warda."

Storyteller:
Everybody in the courtroom began to laugh, and the judge said,

Judge:
So why did you not get out of his way? Do I need to tell you that a sensible man gets out of the way when he hears the cry "warda"? Venice can exist without conceited noblemen, but it cannot exist without honest carriers.

I order you to pay a fine of one hundred gold pieces to this man, who has suffered humiliation, anxiety, and loss of income through your thoughtless actions. And remember the words of King Solomon: "Those who plot evil shall wander away and be lost. But those who plan good shall be granted mercy and quietness."

Storyteller:
I do not know if the nobleman took the judge's words to heart, but Giovanni became even more beloved when he went home. The hundred gold pieces freed him from working sixteen hours a day, and gave him more time to help the poor.

The End

❖

The Clever Maid

A Story About the Values of Cooperation and Responsibility

Characters: *Storyteller, Farmer, Daughter, King, and Peasant.*

Storyteller:
Long ago a poor farmer tried to remove a tree stump from one of his acres, when suddenly his spade hit something hard. Digging carefully he found a golden pot. He ran home as fast as he could, and showing the treasure to his daughter, he cried happily,

Farmer:
The king will reward me if I bring him this golden pot.

Storyteller:
But the daughter shook her head and replied,

Daughter:
Oh no, Papa. Keep the pot and stay out of trouble. If the king sees the golden pot he will insist that you bring him the lid.

Storyteller:
But the father did not listen to his daughter. He ran to the king and said,

Farmer:
Your Majesty, I found this golden pot on my acre, and I want you to have it.

Storyteller:
The king was delighted, but just as the daughter had foreseen he said,

King:
My dear farmer, where there is a pot there must be a lid. If you don't bring me the lid I shall throw you into the dungeon.

Storyteller:
The farmer could not believe his ears. He fell on his knees and wailed,

Farmer:

Oh, what a fool I was. I should have listened to my clever daughter. She told me you would ask for the lid.

Storyteller:

The king looked surprised and replied,

King:

My good man, if your daughter told you what I would say she is indeed a clever woman. I like bright people, and I shall test her cleverness.

Storyteller:

He went into his royal pantry and returned with a basketful of eggs. Handing the basket to the farmer he said,

King:

Here are thirty hard-boiled eggs. Take them home and have your daughter hatch thirty chickens within three days. If she succeeds, she will be rewarded. If she doesn't, I shall punish you for bragging.

Storyteller:

The farmer cried all the way home, but when he handed his daughter the eggs and told her what the king had said, she laughed and replied,

Daughter:

Oh Papa, do not despair. The king is bored, and all he wants to do is to match wits. I think that might be fun. Here, take this pot of boiled beans and tell the king if he can sow them and make them grow, I shall bring him thirty chickens from thirty hard-boiled eggs.

Storyteller:

When the farmer returned with the beans, and his daughter's message, the king laughed heartily. But then he reached into his pocket and gave the farmer a wad of cotton, saying,

King:

Have your clever daughter spin the cotton and weave a sail for my royal sailboat.

Storyteller:

When the daughter saw the cotton she handed her father a small piece of fine wood and said,

Daughter:

Papa, I am sorry you have to do so much running, but something good might come from it. Tell the king that as soon as he makes a spindle

and a weaving chair from this piece of wood, I shall make a sail for
his boat from the wad of cotton he so graciously sent to me.

Storyteller:

The king was highly amused when he got the daughter's message. He
gave the father a small cup and said,

King:

Have your daughter empty out the ocean with this cup and water the
desert.

Storyteller:

The daughter smiled and said to her father,

Daughter:

I am wise and the king is clever.
We could play this game forever.
    Tell the king the minute he stops the flow of all the rivers I will
come and empty the ocean and water the desert.

Storyteller:

The king grinned and said,

King:

This girl is more fun than all my councillors and wise men. I will go
and marry her.

Storyteller:

Thinking that the poor farmer's daughter would be delighted to
marry him, the king went to her farmhouse and said,

King:

I came to marry you, my clever little maid.

Storyteller:

Much to his surprise the girl replied coolly,

Daughter:

I am not your clever little maid, and I will only marry you if you agree
to a prenuptial contract.

Storyteller:

Nothing like that had ever happened to the king. He turned beet red
and shouted,

King:

A prenuptial contract! A poor farmer's daughter is asking me for a
prenuptial contract. Now I have heard everything.

Storyteller:

But the girl curtsied and laughed,

Daughter:

Take it or leave it. I'd rather live with a fair man in a woodshed than with a bully in a castle.

Storyteller:

No one had ever spoken to the king like that. Wondering what she would write, he told her to go ahead, and the girl sat down and wrote:

I agree to become the wife of the king, but should he ever get tired of me and send me away, he must allow me to take along the one thing I value most.

Storyteller:

After reading the contract the king smiled and said,

King:

I must insist on equal rights. I too have something to ask for.

Storyteller:

With a twinkle in her eyes, the girl replied,

Daughter:

Now we are on the right road. What is it you wish?

Storyteller:

The king took the pen and wrote, "The wife I marry must promise never to interfere with my state affairs." The girl thought that was fair enough, and the two of them got married. For quite a while they lived happily, but one day a peasant came to the king and said,

Peasant:

Your Majesty, I meant to sell one of my pregnant cows at the market. During the night she had her calf, but the calf ran over to my neighbor's stall and lay down next to his mare. Now my neighbor claims that his mare gave birth to my calf.

Storyteller:

The king, who was on his way to the forest, replied impatiently,

King:

The calf belongs to the one in whose stall it has been found.

Storyteller:

The peasant was very upset, and because he was related to the queen he went to her and told her his story. At first the queen would not have anything to do with it, but when she remembered how kind her relative had been to her when she was young and poor, she said,

Queen:

Listen carefully. Tomorrow the king is going to review the troops on the market square. Take a rod and a fishing line and pretend you are fishing at the market. When the king asks you why you are fishing on dry land, say this: "If a horse can give birth to a calf, a man can fish on dry land."

Storyteller:

The next day the king went to the market square. Seeing the peasant fishing on dry land, he asked,

King:

Why are you fishing on dry land?

Storyteller:

The peasant replied,

Peasant:

If a horse can give birth to a calf, a man can fish on dry land.

Storyteller:

The king saw that he had made a foolish judgment about the calf, but he also knew that it wasn't the peasant who had come up with the bright answer. He went home to his wife and said furiously,

King:

You broke your promise not to interfere with my state affairs, and for that I shall divorce you and send you back to your father.

Storyteller:

Looking very sad, the queen replied,

Queen:

Dear husband, I admit that I interfered and I am sorry. You are right to send me away, but let us not part as enemies. I am just cooking your favorite meal. Let us eat it together, and then I will leave.

Storyteller:

Because the king could never resist his wife's fine cooking, he sat down and ate and drank, and ate and drank some more. At last the queen served a bottle of the rarest and strongest wine from the king's cellars, and soon the king was snoring like a bear.

Glad that she had learned to carry heavy sacks at her father's farm, the queen wrapped him into a quilted cloth bag and carried him all the way home. When the king awoke the following morning, he found himself in a strange bed. He called for his servants, but none came. Instead his wife entered the room, dressed in a simple but very becoming peasant dress. She sat by his side and said,

Queen:

Forgive me for taking the liberty to remove you from your palace, but I ask you to remember our prenuptial contract. It allows me to take what I value most in case of a divorce, and since there is nothing or no one I value more than you, I took you.

Storyteller:

The king began to laugh like he had never laughed before. He pushed his feather bed away, gave the queen a hearty kiss, and said,

King:

A wise wife is the crown of her husband. I would be the world's biggest fool if I divorced you.

Storyteller:

She kissed him back, and then they ate the delicious peasant breakfast she had prepared. Afterward they returned to the castle, but from then on, whenever the king had a particularly difficult decision to make, he always consulted with his clever and wise wife.

The End

The Clever Village Magistrate
A Story About the Values of Honesty and Respect

Characters: *Storyteller, Merchant, Priest, Peasant, and Magistrate.*

Storyteller:

A wealthy merchant, who lived in a small town in Hessia, decided to visit an annual fair in the city of Frankfurt. On the eve of his departure he took a leather purse, put eight hundred gold pieces into it, and sewed the opening together so the money would not spill out. The following morning he put the leather purse into his saddlebag and took off.

Since it was a long journey the merchant had to spend many nights in the village guest houses along the way. One Saturday evening he got into the company of some weekend revelers and looked too deeply into the bottle. The following morning he put his purse into his saddlebag, but his mind was so befuddled that he failed to close the saddlebag properly.

By the time he stopped at the next village and became aware of his carelessness, the purse was gone. After cursing God and the world for his misfortune he turned around and retraced his path, hoping against hope that he would find his purse. But luck was not with him.

By the time the merchant entered the village where he had been the night before, the church bells were ringing and people were coming out of their houses to go to church. Seeing all those people gave the unhappy man an idea. He rode up to the church, tied his horse to a post, and waited by the door.

When the priest arrived the merchant grabbed him by his sleeve and cried,

Merchant:

Dear Reverend Father, I lost a leather purse with eight hundred gold pieces between this village and the village down the road. If any of your parishioners found it, I am willing to pay a reward of one hundred gold pieces.

Storyteller:

The priest led the merchant inside his church and said to his congregation,

Priest:

> This merchant lost a leather purse with eight hundred gold pieces in it. He promises a reward of one hundred gold pieces to the finder. If one of you found it, I ask you to remember that the Proverbs say, "It is better to be poor and honest than rich and dishonest."

Storyteller:

> The priest had hardly finished his sentence when a young peasant stepped forward and said,

Peasant:

> I have the leather purse. I found it as I was driving my cows to pasture early this morning, and I came to church to ask if someone had lost it. I will get the purse as soon as the service is over.

Storyteller:

> The merchant shook the peasant's hand in gratitude, and after church was over the peasant went home to get the purse. While he was gone the merchant began to regret that he had promised such a large reward.
>
> When the young peasant returned and handed him the purse, the merchant stepped aside and ripped the seam open. As he counted the money, he secretly slipped one hundred gold pieces into the side pockets of his long mantle. When he was done he returned to the peasant and said,

Merchant:

> My dear friend, I see that you have already taken your reward.

Storyteller:

> The peasant looked astonished and said,

Peasant:

> I do not understand what you are talking about.

Storyteller:

> The merchant smiled and replied,

Merchant:

> There is no need to be upset. As you heard I had eight hundred gold pieces in this purse and now there are seven hundred, so you must have taken your reward.

Storyteller:

> The peasant shook his head and replied,

Peasant:

I returned the purse as I found it, and I resent that you are accusing
me of theft. Come, let's bring this case before our village magistrate.

Storyteller:

The merchant did not want to go, but the peasant grabbed him by the
arm and marched him to the magistrate's house. When they arrived
the peasant said,

Peasant:

Your Honor, this morning I drove my cows to pasture. On the way I
found a brown leather purse. I picked it up, but I could not look inside
because the opening was carefully stitched together. However, from
the sound of jingling that came from within, I knew it must be a
money purse.

I took it home and asked my neighbors if they had lost a purse.
When I found out that none of them had, I went to church to ask the
rest of the villagers. After I arrived this man came. He told the priest
that he had lost a money purse with eight hundred gold pieces in it
and that he was willing to give a reward of one hundred gold pieces
to the finder.

I was happy that I had found it, but my joy to be of service to
another human being was short-lived. After I gave the purse to this
man, he undid the stitches, counted the money, and claimed that I
had taken my reward ahead of time.

According to my rules of conduct that would be stealing, and
since I have never stolen a nickel, I resent his accusation and I want
my name cleared.

Storyteller:

After the peasant had finished his story the magistrate said to the
merchant,

Magistrate:

It's your turn to tell me your side of the story.

Storyteller:

The merchant bowed deeply and said,

Merchant:

Your Honor, I lost a purse with eight hundred gold pieces. Because
this man returned my purse with only seven hundred gold pieces I
assume that he has already taken his reward. I'll be glad to have the
money counted so everyone will know that I am telling the truth.

Storyteller:

The magistrate looked at the two men and replied,

Magistrate:

There is no need to count the money if both of you are willing to swear that you are telling the truth and nothing but the truth.

Storyteller:

Both men agreed and swore that they were telling the truth. After the ceremony had taken place the magistrate said,

Magistrate:

Merchant, the Proverbs say, "Some men enjoy cheating, but the cake they buy with such ill-gotten gain will turn to gravel in their mouth." I have known this peasant since he was a small boy and know that he would never tell a lie.

But since you swore that you told the truth and nothing but the truth I must believe you, too. So listen carefully to what I have to say. Since you lost a purse with eight hundred gold pieces, and the peasant found a purse with only seven hundred gold pieces, the purse cannot be yours.

Give the purse with the seven hundred gold pieces to me, and go and find the man who found your purse with the eight hundred gold pieces. In the meantime I will keep the purse with the seven hundred gold pieces for one year. If no one shows up during that year who can prove to me beyond a shadow of a doubt that he is the owner of the purse, the purse will go to the peasant.

Storyteller:

The merchant's face turned as red as a rooster's comb, and he shouted,

Merchant:

But it is my purse. I swear it is my purse.

Storyteller:

The magistrate glared at him and replied,

Magistrate:

You have the right to appeal, but before you take this case to a city judge let me remind you that perjury is a punishable crime, and he who commits it can end up in prison for quite a long time.

Storyteller:

The merchant gulped and replied,

Merchant:

I accept your judgment.

Storyteller:
As he left the courtroom the magistrate turned to the scribe and said:

Magistrate:
Write this story down so the children will learn why,
It's better to tell the truth, than to tell a lie.

The End

The Wicked Judge

A Story About the Values of Responsibility and Humanity

Characters: *Storyteller, Stranger, Judge, Man, Pig, Nun, Orphans, Bad Little Boy, and Old Woman.*

Storyteller:
> A wicked judge left his city one morning to check up on his vineyard workers. On his way home he met a well-dressed stranger. He stopped him and said arrogantly,

Judge:
> I run this city, and you must tell me who you are.

Storyteller:
> The stranger glared at the judge and replied,

Stranger:
> My name is of no consequence, but may it be known to you that today I have permission from someone higher than you and me to take anything that is freely given to me.

Storyteller:
> The judge grinned maliciously and snarled,

Judge:
> I think I know who you are, and I shall come with you to see that you don't take anything unrightfully.

Storyteller:
> They walked back to the city and met a man who was trying to drive a pig to the market. But the pig ran hither and yon, and finally the man cried in a fury at the pig,

Man:
> You nasty pig! I wish the evil one would come and take you.

Storyteller:
> The judge laughed and said to the stranger,

Judge:
> There, you have something that was freely given to you.

119

Storyteller:

But the stranger shook his head and replied,

Stranger:

The man did not mean what he said. He would suffer greatly if I took him at his word.

Storyteller:

After a while they met a nun who was taking a group of orphan children to the park. On the way they passed a pothole filled with water. All the children walked carefully around it. Only one jumped into the pothole, splattering dirty water over everybody. The poor nun cried out,

Nun:

You bad little boy, you ruined everyone's clothes. I just know that one of these days the evil one will come and get you.

Storyteller:

The judge smirked and said to the stranger,

Judge:

She means for you to take him right now.

Storyteller:

The stranger shook his head and replied,

Stranger:

No, she doesn't. She has dedicated her life to those children, and she is trying her best to keep them out of my clutches.

Storyteller:

After a while they passed an old house. An old woman, surrounded by a few shabby household goods, sat in front of it. When she saw the judge she jumped up and cried,

Old Woman:

There goes the wicked judge who evicted me because I could not pay my taxes. He is a terrible curse to all the poor people in this city. Oh how I wish that the evil one would come and get him.

Storyteller:

The judge began to tremble, and he stuttered,

Judge:

She is old, she does not mean what she said.

Storyteller:

But the stranger laughed and shouted,

Stranger:

You and I know that she meant what she said. Come with me, you evil man. It is for you that I came to this town.

Storyteller:

And he grabbed the judge like a hawk grabs a chicken and carried him away.

The End

The Dishonest Innkeeper

A Story About the Value of Honesty

Characters: *Storyteller, Farmer, Farmer's Wife, Innkeeper, and Cattle Dealer.*

Storyteller:

There once lived a good and hard-working farmer who supported his family by raising cattle. However one year the dreaded hoof-and-mouth disease killed his whole herd, and as a result left him close to ruin.

In order to restock, he took his savings of one hundred dollars, borrowed another hundred dollars from his wife's brother, and got ready to visit an animal fair at the nearest market town. On the evening before he left, his wife said,

Farmer's Wife:

Dear husband, I have heard that there are plenty of thieves at those fairs. Watch that no one steals your purse out of your pocket.

Storyteller:

The farmer gave her a hug and chuckled,

Farmer:

Must you always worry? I am a grown man. I'll watch out for my money and myself.

Storyteller:

But he listened to his wife's advice and pinned his pockets shut before he left early the next morning. After walking all day he arrived at the market town and found a bed at a respectable-looking inn.

The following morning, while he was waiting for breakfast, he glanced out of the window and saw all kinds of sinister-looking people leaning against walls and standing in doorways. Remembering his wife's words he became worried and said to himself,

Farmer:

What if my wife is right and someone hits me over the head and steals all my money? I better not take all of it to the market.

Storyteller:

But where was he to leave it? While he was worrying and wondering, the innkeeper, a nice, friendly looking fellow, stepped up to his table and said,

Innkeeper:

A good morning to you, my friend. What can I serve you for breakfast?

Storyteller:

The farmer ordered eggs and ham, and while the innkeeper went to get it he looked around and thought,

Farmer:

This is a respectable, established inn, and there are other guests here. Surely they would not be here if the innkeeper were a dishonest man. I will ask him to safeguard one hundred dollars for me, and I'll take the other hundred for earnest money in case I find a herd that suits me.

Storyteller:

When it was time to pay for breakfast he asked the innkeeper to step aside and said,

Farmer:

Good innkeeper, I am here to buy a herd of cattle, but looking around I find that it might be wiser not to carry too much money with me. Could I please leave one hundred dollars with you?

Storyteller:

The innkeeper replied,

Innkeeper:

My good friend, you are a wise man. Many of my guests leave their money with me. I will put it into my strongbox and give it back to you as soon as you need it.

Storyteller:

Glad that he had solved his problem, the farmer counted out one hundred dollars and left. As soon as he came to the market he found a dealer who had a fine herd of cattle for sale. After a bit of haggling they agreed that the final price should be two hundred dollars.

The farmer paid one hundred dollars in earnest money and went back to the inn. There he sought out the innkeeper and said happily,

Farmer:

Dear innkeeper, I found a fine herd and I have come for my money.

Storyteller:

The innkeeper stared at him as if he had never seen him before and replied,

Innkeeper:

What money are you talking about?

Storyteller:

The farmer looked astonished and replied,

Farmer:

I am talking about the money I left with you this morning.

Storyteller:

The innkeeper shook his head and said,

Innkeeper:

My friend, you must be confused. I remember you paid your bill, but I can assure you that you did not leave any money with me.

Storyteller:

By now the farmer, who knew perfectly well that he had left half of his money with the innkeeper, became angry and shouted,

Farmer:

I know I left half of my money with you, and I want you to return it to me right now.

Storyteller:

His shouting did not worry the innkeeper at all. Smiling coldly, he replied,

Innkeeper:

My good countryman, do you have a witness? Only fools give away large sums of money without a reliable witness. Now go and bother me no more or else I will have you arrested for disturbing the peace and making false accusations.

Storyteller:

What could the farmer do but leave. Furious with himself that he had been so trusting, he ran out into the street, tearing his hair in despair. After a while he went back to the dealer. Seeing at once that something was seriously wrong, the dealer asked,

Cattle Dealer:

You look like you have seen a ghost. What has happened?

Storyteller:

The farmer replied bitterly,

Farmer:

The deal is off. I am a ruined man. Fearing thieves and pickpockets, I left half of my money with the innkeeper, but when I came back and asked for it, the scoundrel claimed he had no idea what I was talking about.

Storyteller:

The dealer raised his eyebrow and asked,

Cattle Dealer:

Didn't you have a witness when you gave the innkeeper your money?

Storyteller:

The farmer shook his head and replied,

Farmer:

No, I was a fool. But where I come from, the word of an honest man is as good as a thousand witnesses. Should you now refuse to give me back my earnest money I will have to sell my farm to pay off my debt, and my family and I will have to go begging.

Storyteller:

The dealer laughed and said,

Cattle Dealer:

Here is your money. A fortune can be made from cheating, but there is a curse that goes with it. I don't make a living cheating others out of their hard-earned money, but let me think: I am sure there is a way to get your money back.

Storyteller:

The farmer could not believe his ears. Here was a man willing to help him when he thought the whole world had turned against him. Offering his hand to the dealer, he replied,

Farmer:

I am ready to try anything.

Storyteller:

After listening to the dealer's plan the two men separated and walked back to the inn. The dealer entered first and ordered a glass of beer. The farmer entered a few minutes later and went straight to the innkeeper and said with a trembling voice,

Farmer:

Innkeeper, I am sorry I spoke so roughly to you this morning. I am not used to a big town, and I am afraid I have become rather confused. All I know is that my money is gone, and I ask you to please tell me, are you absolutely sure that I didn't leave a hundred dollars in your keeping?

Storyteller:

The innkeeper replied,

Innkeeper:

You probably meant to leave your money with me, but I swear you didn't.

Storyteller:

The farmer shook his head in bewilderment and asked,

Farmer:

What could have happened? I can't imagine that a pickpocket took my money. I pinned my pockets shut.

Storyteller:

The innkeeper sniggered and replied,

Innkeeper:

Most pickpockets are so skilled at what they are doing they will steal an egg from under a brooding hen without her knowing it.

Storyteller:

Pretending to be frightened, the farmer looked around and whispered,

Farmer:

If that happened I am afraid that they will steal my remaining money, too, and unless I buy at least a few cattle I will be a ruined man. Please, dear innkeeper, safeguard the rest of my money until I have made a new deal.

Storyteller:

Wiping a grin off his face, the innkeeper agreed, and the farmer took out his money. But before he gave it to the innkeeper he walked over to the dealer and said,

Farmer:

Sir, I will pay for your beer if you would be so kind as to be a witness to a money transaction.

Storyteller:

The dealer agreed, and after he had witnessed the transaction he hurried away. The farmer followed the dealer to the fairground, and they sat down and talked about cattle and farms and how hard it was to make a living. A little while later the farmer went without the dealer to the innkeeper and said,

Farmer:

Innkeeper, I found some fine cattle and I need my money.

Storyteller:

The innkeeper said to himself,

Innkeeper:

I must not keep his second hundred dollars because this time he had a witness.

Storyteller:

He went to his strongbox, gave the farmer the money, and the farmer left. A quarter of an hour later the farmer returned with the witness. Acting like he hadn't seen the innkeeper fifteen minutes before, he said,

Farmer:

Ah, my dear friend, I struck a fine bargain. Give me back the hundred dollars I asked you to keep for me.

Storyteller:

This time it was the turn of the innkeeper to look confused. He stared at the farmer and said,

Innkeeper:

Didn't I see you just a few minutes ago?

Storyteller:

The farmer looked astonished and replied,

Farmer:

Not that I know. I was out bargaining for my cattle.

Storyteller:

Realizing that he had been outwitted, the innkeeper had no choice but to give the rest of the money back. In order to save face he said to the farmer and the dealer-witness,

Innkeeper:

My dear friends, won't you celebrate your transaction by having dinner at my place?

Storyteller:

Both the farmer and the dealer grinned and said in one accord,

Farmer and Cattle Dealer:

Not at your place, dear honest innkeeper.

Storyteller:

Laughing at the dumbfounded face of the villain, they linked arms and went across the street to the innkeeper's competitor. After they had eaten a hearty dinner they bought a bottle of wine for the rest of the guests and told them what had happened.

Word got around, and soon other people who had also been cheated by that innkeeper came forth and told their stories. Less than a year later the dishonest innkeeper was forced to close his inn and leave town.

The End

Part III
Stories That Involve the Audience

Storyteller Annette Harrison says this about stories that involve the audience, "My greatest joy is when my voice combines with a chorus of young voices to sing and chant together. We jump into a story, become the characters, relive the adventures, and rejoice in the experience."

When my own children were young I told them a lot of stories. One day my husband made us a set of homemade puppets, and I began to use them in the stories. For example, when there was a king in the story I picked up the king-puppet and had him say the story king's lines.

Because there often was dialogue between more than two story characters I asked my children to help. We decided at the beginning of the story who would play the king, queen, princess, and so on, and, as I told the story, the children held their puppets and repeated or paraphrased their characters' lines.

When my children grew older I took my puppets and stories into the St. Louis schools. Dealing with more children, less room, and limited time I had to plan my stories very carefully. I learned it was easiest to seat the main characters in order of their appearance on a row of chairs facing the class, and have them use that area to move around and interact with each other.

To help children understand what I want them to do I often draw seating diagrams on the chalkboard and explain how I want everyone to move as we act out the story. (See "Bunny Pink Learns How to Think," page 131.)

Adding rhymes and songs for the rest of the children keeps everyone involved and turns our stories into the same plays as you find in this part of the book.

"Bunny Pink" is an easy-to-learn Easter story. It has a lot of repetitions and gives young children a chance to show off their counting skills. Because the rhymes in the story of Old Man Winter and Rabbit Mother are a bit harder to remember, I write them on the chalkboard and teach them to the children before we begin the play.

Puppets are optional, but I can't sing their praises loudly enough. Puppets do miracles for people of all ages. It is much easier to persuade a shy kindergartner or a self-conscious teenager to take part in a story with a puppet than without.

Here is an easy way to make puppets:

1. Have the children draw the appropriate pictures of the story characters or cut them from magazines.

2. Laminate them several times.

3. Glue a popsicle stick to the back, and, voilà, you have a puppet.

Bunny Pink Learns How to Think

A Story About the Values of Self-Esteem and Responsibility

Characters: *Storyteller, Easter Bunny, Bunny Pink, Old Hen, Mother Earth, Father Sky, Cloud Woman, and Wind Bird*

Props: A basket with ten decorated construction paper eggs, each with the name of your choice on it.

Action: Holding their puppets in their hands the main players sit in a row and repeat their lines after the storyteller. Bunny Pink moves around chairs as storyteller directs and arrows indicate.

→ → → → → → → → → → → → →
Easter Bunny. Bunny Pink. Old Hen. Mother Earth. Father Sky. Cloud Woman. Wind Bird.
← ← ← ← ← ← ← ← ← ← ← ←

The rest of the children face main players and participate as the storyteller chants, claps hands, and dances.

Storyteller:
One fine day Mother Rabbit gave birth to a beautiful bunny rabbit. She named him Bunny Pink because the insides of his lovely long ears looked like pink velvet.

A year later Easter Bunny called Bunny Pink to his side and said,

Easter Bunny:
Bunny Pink, Easter is coming, and I have heard good things about you. Tell me, how high can you count?

Storyteller:
Bunny Pink smiled proudly and replied,

Bunny Pink:
I can count all the way up to ten.

Storyteller:

Easter Bunny smiled and said,

Easter Bunny:

Good for you, Bunny Pink. If you can count to ten you are ready to help us with the Easter eggs. Go to the storage house, fetch ten eggs and the names of ten children. Color those eggs as well as you can and deliver them to the children on Easter morning.

Storyteller:

Bunny Pink was delighted. He got the eggs and the names, and he colored the eggs as carefully as he could. It took him a long time, but by the time he put the eggs into his Easter egg delivery basket, he was proud of his work. (*Put eggs into basket.*)

The first one was a sky blue egg for Daniel. The second one was a yellow egg for Christina. The third one was a red egg for Patrick. The fourth one was a green egg for Stephanie. The fifth one was a purple egg for Miriam. The sixth one was a blue egg with white polka dots for Laura. The seventh one was a yellow egg with orange stripes for Kate. The eighth one was a purple egg for little Nickolaus. The ninth one was a blue and red egg for Henry. The tenth one was a pink egg for Valerie.

All of them were done to perfection, and Bunny Pink was sure Easter Bunny would be proud of him. Bunny Pink rested on Friday, but on Saturday, just to make sure that everything was right, he decided to count the eggs again.

One, two, three, four, five, six, seven, eight, nine. Oh no! The tenth egg was missing. Bunny Pink counted them again and again until he finally had to admit to himself that the tenth egg was gone. What could have happened? Did a squirrel or a rat sneak into the storeroom and take it? They were known to do things like that.

Bunny Pink began to cry. He cried and cried until he realized that it was of no use to sit and cry. He had to go to Easter Bunny and tell him what had happened. All upset he hopped over to Easter Bunny's house and said,

Bunny Pink:

Oh Easter Bunny, please help me, I don't have an egg for Valerie.

Storyteller:

Easter Bunny looked aghast, and he said,

Easter Bunny:

You don't have an egg for Valerie? What happened?

Storyteller:

Bunny Pink's eyes grew misty, and he whispered tearfully,

Bunny Pink:
> I don't know. The egg just disappeared. I know I had a tenth egg. I even remember how I colored it.

Storyteller:
> Easter Bunny thought for a while, and then he said sternly,

Easter Bunny:
> Bunny Pink, I can't help you. You have to solve this problem yourself, or you will never be a proper Easter bunny. Now go and don't waste time. There are only a few hours left before Easter morning.

Storyteller:
> Poor Bunny Pink began to think, and suddenly he had an idea. He said to himself,

Bunny Pink:
> I need to find a hen who will lay just one more egg for me.

Storyteller:
> Once Bunny Pink knew what to do he followed Easter Bunny's advice, and he didn't waste any time. (*As Bunny Pink hops twice around the block of chairs, the children chant with the storyteller:*)
>> He hopped and he hopped and he never stopped,
>> And he hopped and he hopped and he never stopped,
>> until he found a henhouse. (*Bunny Pink sits down.*)
>
> But when he entered the henhouse, he found all the hens sound asleep. I must wake them up, thought Bunny Pink, and he yelled at the top of his voice,

Bunny Pink:
> Hens, dear hens, wake up and help me.
> I need one more egg for Valerie.

Storyteller (*tells hens' part*):
> But the hens muttered, "Bok, bok, bok, bok we can't help you. We are plumb exhausted from laying all those eggs for Easter. Come back in a week, and we might be able to lay another egg or two."
> But Bunny Pink pleaded,

Bunny Pink:
> Dear hens, I can't wait that long. I need an egg right now. Please be so kind and understand that all children who celebrate Easter will get an Easter egg. Only Valerie will be empty-handed, and how can I explain to a little girl that I don't know what happened to her Easter egg?

Storyteller *(tells hens' part)*:

But all his pleading didn't help. The hens clucked, "No, no, no, no," and went back to sleep. Only one old hen, who had lived a bit longer and knew more about the ways of the world, muttered,

Old Hen:

If you feed me a worm I might gain the strength to lay just one more egg.

Storyteller:

There was a ray of hope. Bunny Pink began to think for the second time. Mother Earth would give him a worm. Once he knew what to do Bunny Pink didn't waste any time. *(Children join in.)*

He hopped and he hopped and he never stopped,
And he hopped and he hopped and he never stopped,
until he came to Mother Earth.

When he arrived Bunny Pink bowed and said,

Bunny Pink:

Mother Earth, Mother Earth, please give me a juicy worm so I can take it to Old Hen, so she can lay an egg, so I can put it into my basket and bring it to Valerie on Easter morning.

Storyteller:

But Mother Earth shook her head and said sadly,

Mother Earth:

Dear Bunny Pink, I would love to give you a juicy worm so you can take it to the old hen, but look how dry and hard my surface is. No worm will ever find its way out.

Storyteller:

Bunny Pink began to think for the third time. He said to Mother Earth,

Bunny Pink:

If I hop to Father Sky and ask him to send you some rain, will you give me a worm?

Storyteller:

Mother Earth nodded, and Bunny Pink didn't waste any time. *(Children join in.)*

He hopped and he hopped and he never stopped,
And he hopped and he hopped and he never stopped,
until he came to Father Sky.

When he arrived he bowed and said,

Bunny Pink:

>Father Sky, Father Sky, please send Mother Earth some rain so she can give me a worm, so I can take it to Old Hen, so she can lay an egg, so I can put it into my basket and bring it to Valerie on Easter morning.

Storyteller:

>But Father Sky shook his head and said sadly,

Father Sky:

>I would love to send Mother Earth some rain, but I am blue today. I think all my clouds are with Cloud Woman.

Storyteller:

>Bunny Pink began to think for the fourth time. He said to Father Sky,

Bunny Pink:

>If I hop over to Cloud Woman and ask her to send you some clouds will you make them rain?

Storyteller:

>When Father Sky nodded, Bunny Pink didn't waste any time. *(Children join in.)*
>>He hopped and he hopped and he never stopped,
>>And he hopped and he hopped and he never stopped,
>>until he came to Cloud Woman.
>
>When he arrived he bowed and said,

Bunny Pink:

>Cloud Woman, Cloud Woman, please send some clouds to Father Sky so he can send some rain to Mother Earth, so Mother Earth can give me a worm, so I can take it to Old Hen, so she can lay an egg, so I can put it into my basket and bring it to Valerie on Easter morning.

Storyteller:

>But Cloud Woman shook her head and said sadly,

Cloud Woman:

>I would love to give you clouds so you can take them to Father Sky, but I took a nap and they left while I was sleeping.

Storyteller:

>For the fifth time Bunny Pink began to think, and suddenly he had an idea. He said to Cloud Woman,

Bunny Pink:

>If I go and ask Wind Bird to find them, will you be able to send them to Father Sky?

Storyteller:

When Cloud Woman nodded, Bunny Pink didn't waste any time. *(Children join in.)*

> He hopped and he hopped and he never stopped,
> And he hopped and he hopped and he never stopped,
> until he came to Wind Bird.

When he arrived he bowed and said,

Bunny Pink:

Wind Bird, dear Wind Bird, please find the clouds and blow them to Cloud Woman so she can send them to Father Sky, so he can send some rain to Mother Earth, so Mother Earth can give me a worm, so I can take it to Old Hen, so she can lay an egg, so I can put it into my basket and bring it to Valerie on Easter morning.

Storyteller:

Wind Bird smiled and replied,

Wind Bird:

I like Valerie. For her I will find the clouds and blow them over to Cloud Woman.

Storyteller:

Bunny Pink hopped up and down with excitement, and he shouted,

Bunny Pink:

How can I ever thank you?

Storyteller:

Wind Bird chuckled,

Wind Bird:

There is no need to thank me. We are in this world to help one another.

Storyteller:

Wind Bird found the clouds, and he puffed up his cheeks and blew the clouds to Cloud Woman, *(Children play clouds and twirl around and sing),*

> Swishswishsssssssssssss,
> swashsssssssssssss,

who sent them to Father Sky, who made them rain on Mother Earth. *(Children sit down, clap hands, and chant)*

> Pitter patter, pitter patter,
> Watch it splatter, watch it splatter.
> Watch it rain, watch it rain.
> Soon it will be dry again.

Mother Earth gave Bunny Pink a worm. *(Children wiggle like worms.)*
 Wiggle, wiggle, wiggle, wiggle.

Bunny Pink took it to Old Hen, who swallowed it and laid an egg.
(Children join in.)
 Bok, bok, bok, bok, bok.

Full of happiness Bunny Pink took the egg home. But the egg that the old hen laid was white, and when Bunny Pink went to paint it he saw that all of the paint pots were empty.

 For the sixth time Bunny Pink began to think, and suddenly he had an idea. He checked the brushes and found there was just enough paint left in each one to paint the most beautiful design on Valerie's egg.

 By the time he was finished the sun had risen, and Bunny Pink joined Easter Bunny and all the other bunny rabbits and brought Easter eggs to all the children who were waiting for them.

 All of the bunnies had fun, but none of them was as happy as Bunny Pink. When he put Valerie's egg into her basket, he felt like singing and shouting with gladness, because he had managed to solve his problem all by himself.

 And what did Valerie say when she found her egg? She said, "Wowee!" and she peeled it and ate it.

The End

Old Man Winter and
Rabbit Mother
A Story About the Values of Responsibility and Perseverance

Characters: *Storyteller, Old Man Winter, Jack Frost, Rabbit Mother, Big Wolf, Fox, Old Bear, Cacaw the Crow, and Birds*

Props: Construction paper eggs.

Action: Holding their puppets in their hands the main players sit in a row and repeat their lines after the storyteller. Rabbit Mother moves around chairs as storyteller directs and arrows indicate. Because we don't use a stage I don't worry about puppet manipulation.

→ → → → → → → → → → → → →

Old Man Winter. J. Frost. Rabbit Mother. Big Wolf. Fox. Old Bear. Crow.

← ← ← ← ← ← ← ← ← ← ← ← ←

C   N

  H   E

     I   L   D   R

The rest of the children face main players and double as birds and chorus. Because the rhymes in this story are rather long I usually write them on the chalkboard and rap them together with the children. The hopping and the dancing are spontaneous.

Storyteller:
> On a cold March morning Old Man Winter stepped out of his ice cave and shouted,

Old Man Winter:
> Jack Frost, Jack Frost, come here. See how beautiful the world looks under the snow white blanket.

Storyteller:
Jack Frost came running and cried,

Jack Frost:
You are right, Old Man Winter. Everything looks so wonderful that I wish it could last forever.

Storyteller:
Old Man Winter sighed deeply and replied,

Old Man Winter:
I wish so, too, Jack Frost, but you and I know that as soon as the first flowers pop their heads out of the ground we have to make room for spring and return to the North Pole.

Storyteller:
Jack Frost wrinkled his forehead and stared for a long time at the snow. Suddenly he hopped three feet high and shouted,

Jack Frost:
Old Man Winter, I have a splendid idea. Why don't you call the North Wind and ask him to blow up a real blizzard. Let him dump five feet of snow on the Earth, and I bet you not a single flower will bloom.

Storyteller:
Old Man Winter's eyes lit up, and he replied,

Old Man Winter:
That is an excellent idea, Jack Frost. If the flowers don't bloom spring can't come, and we can stay here all year long. Let's do it.

Storyteller:
They both began to dance and they shouted *(rapped)*,

Jack Frost and Old Man Winter: *(Children jump around and clap their hands, and rap)*
Come, old North Wind, come and blow,
Blow up a blizzard, so nothing will grow. *(Repeat)*

Storyteller:
Nothing could have pleased the North Wind more than to blow up a blizzard. Soon everyone in the world began to suffer. Flowers couldn't grow. Fathers couldn't go to work. Children couldn't go to school. Mothers couldn't go to grocery stories. Within a very short time all the people in the world were miserable from lack of food and warmth, and no one knew what to do.

But not only the people were in trouble. The poor creatures in the forests and mountains were also cold, hungry, and scared. They would have died but for a brave Rabbit Mother, who lived underneath the roots of an old tree, right next to Old Man Winter's cave.

Rabbit Mother happened to be home the day Old Man Winter and Jack Frost decided to stay all year long. When she heard them invite the North Wind to blow up a blizzard she became very upset. She knew her babies were on the way, and she realized quickly that they would either starve or freeze to death unless someone found a way to make Old Man Winter and Jack Frost leave. But who was going to do it? Rabbit Mother thought and thought, and after a while she said to herself,

Rabbit Mother:
If all the animals in the forest get together, we should be able to find a way to drive Old Man Winter and Jack Frost back to the North Pole.

Storyteller:
Rabbit Mother knew that her friends the chipmunks, the pole cats, the possums, the squirrels, the wild turkeys, the turtles, and the raccoons would be more than willing to help. But they would need the big animals, too, and Rabbit Mother knew she could ask no one but herself to approach them. (*As Rabbit Mother runs around the block of chairs, children clap their hands and rap.*)

So she ran and ran with the swiftest of feet,
over snow and ice, through slush and sleet,
until she came to Big Wolf's den.

Although her heart was beating like a drum, she knocked on the door of Big Wolf's den and cried,

Rabbit Mother:
Big Wolf, Big Wolf, I need to talk to you.

Storyteller:
Big Wolf stepped out of his den and growled,

Big Wolf:
What makes you come here, Rabbit Mother? Aren't you afraid I might eat you?

Storyteller:
Of course Rabbit Mother was afraid, but she couldn't allow herself to think about it. She took a deep breath and said,

Rabbit Mother: *(Children join in.)*
> Big Wolf, the news I bring is bad.
> Old Man Winter has gone stark raving mad.
> He and Jack Frost are planning to stay,
> And we will freeze to death, lest we drive them away.

Storyteller:
> Rabbit Mother thought Big Wolf would offer his help immediately.
> But Big Wolf sneered,

Big Wolf: *(Children join in.)*
> Who cares if those blockheads want to stay.
> I wouldn't move a toe to drive them away.
> I can always find food, and my fur is warm.
> Winter and Frost can do me no harm.
> Now beat it, old Rabbit, before I feel the need,
> To dine on a morsel of rabbit meat.

Storyteller:
> Rabbit Mother got the message. *(Wolf chases her once around block of chairs and sits down.)* She turned on her heels *(Children join in.)*
>> And she ran, and she ran, with the swiftest of feet,
>> Over snow and ice, through slush and sleet,
>> Until she came to Fox's den.
>
> Although her little heart was beating like a drum, she scratched at his door and cried,

Rabbit Mother:
> Mr. Fox, come out, I need to talk to you.

Storyteller:
> Mr. Fox came out of his den, and when he saw Rabbit Mother he mocked,

Fox:
> What makes you come here, Rabbit Mother? I didn't know we had a dinner date.

Storyteller:
> Rabbit Mother tried not to tremble as she cried,

Rabbit Mother: *(Children join in.)*
> Mr. Fox, the news I bring is bad.
> Old Man Winter has gone stark raving mad.
> He and Jack Frost are planning to stay,
> And we will freeze to death, lest we drive them away.

Storyteller:
But Mr. Fox jeered,

Fox: *(Children join in.)*
Who cares if those dimwitties want to stay.
I wouldn't move a toe to drive them away.
I can always find food, and my fur is warm.
Winter and Frost can do me no harm.
Now beat it, old Rabbit, before I feel the need,
To dine on a morsel of rabbit meat.

Storyteller:
Again, Rabbit Mother got the message. *(Fox chases her once around block of chairs.) (Children join in.)*
And she ran, and she ran, with the swiftest of feet,
Over snow and ice, through slush and sleet,
Until she reached Old Bear's den.

She scratched at his door and cried,

Rabbit Mother:
Old Bear, wake up, we are in trouble.

Storyteller:
Old Bear came to the entrance of his den and grumbled,

Old Bear:
It's not spring yet, Rabbit Mother. How dare you wake me up.

Storyteller:
Rabbit Mother hopped up and down and replied,

Rabbit Mother: *(Children join in.)*
Old Bear, the news I bring is bad.
Old Man Winter has gone stark raving mad.
He and Jack Frost are planning to stay,
And we will freeze to death, lest we drive them away.

Storyteller:
Old Bear was a bit gentler in his reply than Big Wolf and Fox. He said,

Old Bear:
You didn't need to come here, Rabbit dear.
You should have known that I have nothing to fear.
I can always find food, and my fur is warm.
Those two old dolts can do me no harm.
Now go away, and don't wake me, I pray,
Unless you have something more important to say.

Storyteller:

Poor Rabbit Mother left and returned to her cold nest. There she sat, and once again she thought and thought. But in spite of all her thinking she didn't have the faintest idea what to do. Suddenly she heard a knock at her door. Rabbit Mother peeked outside and saw her friend Cacaw the crow. Cacaw looked terribly upset, and she sputtered,

Cacaw:

Rabbit Mother, can you tell me what is going on? Isn't it high time for Old Man Winter and Jack Frost to be gone? I just got finished laying my eggs, and I am ready to hatch them. But in this weather they'll freeze.

Storyteller:

Rabbit Mother looked at Cacaw the crow and replied,

Rabbit Mother:

Cacaw, haven't you heard that Old Man Winter and Jack Frost plan to stay forever? Eggs, babies, all of us are doomed to die unless we find a way to drive them back to the North Pole.

Storyteller:

Convinced that Rabbit Mother had lost her senses, Cacaw shouted,

Cacaw:

Rabbit Mother, that's ridiculous. Everyone knows that as soon as the first spring flower pokes her head out of the ground, Old Man Winter and Jack Frost are obliged to leave.

Storyteller:

But Rabbit Mother shook her head and said sadly,

Rabbit Mother:

Not really, Cacaw. Look around. All Old Man Winter needed to do was to order more snow so the flowers couldn't grow. If he keeps on doing that, he and Jack Frost can stay forever and ever.

Storyteller:

Poor Cacaw stared at Rabbit Mother with horror in her eyes, and without another word she flew up to her nest and pitched all her eggs into the snow. Now it was Rabbit Mother's turn to be horrified. She cried,

Rabbit Mother:

Why did you do that, Cacaw?

Storyteller:

Cacaw flapped her wings and cawed furiously,

Cacaw:

Why do you ask, Rabbit Mother? Can't you see that it's of no use to hatch those eggs?

Storyteller:

Rabbit Mother stared sadly at the five lovely eggs. But suddenly she ran up to them and put one egg in the middle and four eggs around it. Excitedly, she turned to Cacaw and cried,

Rabbit Mother:

Cacaw, Cacaw, come and look. Tell me, what do those eggs look like?

Storyteller:

Cacaw came out of her nest and looked and cried,

Cacaw:

You arranged them to look like a flower, Rabbit Mother. I can't believe it. My eggs look like a flower. Maybe if we put a few more eggs next to my eggs we could try to fool Old Man Winter and Jack Frost into leaving.

Storyteller:

Rabbit Mother laughed, and she said,

Rabbit Mother:

Cacaw, that is exactly what I am thinking. Go and tell each of your bird friends to bring me one egg before nightfall. As soon as the moon comes out we will arrange them in the shape of flowers in front of Old Man Winter's cave, and then we all must hope and pray that he and Jack Frost will mistake them for real flowers when they come out tomorrow morning.

Storyteller:

Cacaw flew to the birds' nests, and when the birds heard what Rabbit Mother planned to do, each came with a precious egg. *(Children bring paper eggs.)* They waited till it grew dark, and then they got busy. Quietly, ever so quietly, they sneaked to the meadow in front of Old Man Winter's cave and put the eggs in the shape of flowers on top of the snow.

The following morning Old Man Winter and Jack Frost stepped out of their cave. As usual they meant to feast their eyes on a fine, white, winter landscape. But it was no longer there. The whole meadow in front of the cave was covered with bright dots, and when Old Man Winter saw the bright specks of color he hollered,

Old Man Winter:

Jack Frost, your plan didn't work. I don't know how these flowers made it through the snow, but I do know that it is the sign for us to leave.

Storyteller:

Jack Frost stomped his foot on the ground and shouted,

Jack Frost:

At least no one can say we didn't try.

Storyteller:

And then he grabbed Old Man Winter's hand, and they both marched off to the North Pole singing. (*Old Man Winter and Jack Frost march around chairs and then to back of classroom.*)

Jack Frost and Old Man Winter:

Ho, ho, ho, ho, ho, to the North Pole we will go.
The Earth wants no more ice and snow.
The flowers say it's time to go.
Ho, ho, ho, ho, ho, to the North Pole we will go.

Storyteller:

The minute they were gone the sun came out and melted all the snow. A day later the real flowers poked their little heads out of the ground, and spring arrived in all its glory. Everyone was happy, but none were happier than Rabbit Mother and Cacaw—the two little ones who had outsmarted two big ones.

The End

Notes on the Stories

Part I: Stories to Tell and Read Aloud

The Faithful Wives
This German folktale comes from a collection of folktales and fairy tales by Ludwig Bechstein. There is a similar theme in the story "The Clever Maid."

Mother Holdra's Tonic
This tale comes from the book *Frau Holle*. Frau Holle (Mother Holdra) is one of the most popular characters in the Norse mythology. She lives above the clouds and when she shakes out her featherbed it snows on Earth. In the original story, Katrinele's reward is a ball of yarn that never grows smaller. I changed it to a recipe for an herbal tonic because it provided work for all the poor villagers.

Hideehohee
This is an original story that tells us about the ups and downs in the life of a little elf.

The Giant Who Learned to Love Children
I found the story of the giant Helming in a book of Norse mythology that belonged to my father when he was a child. In the original story the giant is depicted as a dolt, and there are no children.

The Elf's Hat
This fairy tale also comes from the Bechstein collection. In the original version a third son rescues the brothers from the elves, and the elves make a potion for the father.

The Farmer and the Wolf
Peter Paul Hebel was a German collector of fables. I adopted this fable from his book *Treasurebox of Fables*. It teaches that stealing can get one into trouble.

The Three Hundred Iron Rods
This is a fable I read in a German reader for school children that no longer exists.

The King and the Broommaker
King Frederick the Great was one of Germany's most beloved kings. Many stories are told about him, and this is my favorite one. I found it in the book of Prussian fairy tales.

Hans and Grete, Nineteen Now
This story is based on the popular story Hansel and Gretel from *Grimm's Fairy Tales*. I have told it in many schools and in a juvenile detention center. In order to see the students' reactions I asked them to write letters to Hans, Grete, and Crack-Witch.

Bird Baby Don't Fly
This is an original story that attempts to make children see the consequences of certain actions.

The Boy Who Called the King a Fool
This original story teaches us the true horror of war.

A Perjurer Is a Liar
This story was inspired by a story from Bechstein's collection. I added the neighbors, the wife, and the daughter.

The Bridge Across the Fire
This is a Muslim legend that teaches compassion. It comes from the African Epic *Sundiata*.

The Hehheh Tales

Hehheh and the Honey Cakes
This original story teaches a conceited woman humility.

Hehheh and the Magic Needle
My husband remembered the story of 'The Magic Needle' from his German reader. I changed it into a Hehheh story.

Hehheh and the Fisherman
This is an original story that teaches people to keep their promises.

Hehheh and the Hay
This original story teaches that gloating about the misfortunes of others is not the best thing to do, especially when Hehheh is around.

Hehheh and the Mayor
This story was inspired by one of Bechstein's folktales.

Part II: Stories to Act Out

The Three Languages

There are many variations of this story. I use the simpler ones for young children and the more complex ones for older students. I chose a girl to be the heroine and added the greedy nephew. The children delight in making up their own animal languages. As a follow-up activity we talk about the fact that, even nowadays, animals speak to us. For example, birds move away from areas where the pollution level becomes too high for their survival.

The Elephant and the Monkey

This wonderful story teaches children the beauty and wisdom of African tales. I found it in a booklet called *Fables of the Chokosi*.

The Farmer and the Stork

This Aesop fable hopefully teaches children to think twice before they let others persuade them to do foolish things.

Kannitverstan

This story comes from the Peter Paul Hebel collection. It teaches us that all the riches in the world cannot save us from the last road all people must travel.

A Mother's Advice

This story came to me by oral tradition. I added it to this collection because it has a good message and is easy to act out.

The Nobleman and the Carrier

This story comes to us through oral tradition. It takes us to Italy, and, as a follow-up, we talk about customs in other countries.

The Clever Maid

This story comes from Europe. It has many variations and is a wonderful story to act out.

The Clever Village Magistrate

I began to look for stories like this one when I realized that my middle school students like to act out stories that have judges. It comes from the Peter Paul Hebel collection.

The Wicked Judge

This story comes from the Ludwig Bechstein collection and is a warning to ruthless officials who gain wealth by oppressing the poor.

The Dishonest Innkeeper

I adapted this story from a collection of French folktales.

Part III: Stories That Involve the Audience

Bunny Pink Learns How to Think

Here is an Easter story with which the children in the listening audience can play along and learn sequencing skills.

Old Man Winter and Rabbit Mother

This story needs a bit more preparation than the other participation story because the rhymes are longer. But I have found that older children (ages 8-10) learn the rhymes very fast and love to perform the stories for younger children.

About the Author and Illustrator

Ruthilde Kronberg is a storyteller, lecturer, and writer. She involves children in storytelling and in discussions about the messages stories bring. Mrs. Kronberg began her professional storytelling career with Springboard to Learning and enrichment programs in the St. Louis public schools and has also given workshops at numerous colleges and universities in the greater St. Louis area. She is the author of *A Piece of the Wind and Other Stories to Tell* with Patricia C. McKissack (San Francisco: Harper & Row, 1990), co-authored *For the Bible Tells Me So* with Louise Ulmer and Lynn Rubright (St. Louis: Concordia Publishing House, 1979), and contributed to *A Story of Williwu the Lonely Little Rich Girl*, an anthology of audience participation stories compiled by Teresa Miller with the assistance of Ann Pellowisky (Cambridge, Mass.. Yellow Moon Press, 1988). Mrs. Kronberg came to the United States from Germany in 1953. She is married to Peter Kronberg and has four grown children.

Michael Kronberg is an illustrator and graphic designer who lives and works in New York City. This collaboration with his mother is his first book for children.